To Hans Schr...
With thanks,
Herb Wendes

Herb and older brother Rudy

A GERMAN SEED
GROWS IN
AMERICA

*Memoirs of the Trials and Tribulations
of an American Child
Born of German Immigrants*

Herb Wendes

A GERMAN SEED GROWS IN AMERICA
Memoirs of the Trials and Tribulations of an American Child
Born of German Immigrants
Copyright © 2013 by Herb Wendes

Paperback
ISBN 13: 978-1-93763-275-5
ISBN 10: 1-93763-275-X

Library of Congress Control Number: 2013956454

Published by Dark Planet Publishing
www.DarkPlanetPublishing.com

Printed in the United States of America

CONTENTS

Part I
THE SEED SPROUTS OUT

Part II
GROWING UP IN THE SHADE OF THE GERMAN CULTURE

Part III
THE ROOTS AND BRANCHES SPROUT OUT

———

Part IV

BACK ON AMERICAN SOIL

———

Part V

NEIGHBORING TREES AND FELLOW BRANCHES

Part I

THE SEED SPROUTS OUT
*Growing Up in the Depression
and WWII Years*

Chapter 1
RISKS OF A NICKNAME

I t was a sweltering 95 degrees in Chicago on July 1st, 1931 when I entered this world. The event took place in Jackson Park Hospital, on the south side of the city not far from the lakefront. The maternity ward was located on the top floor. The intense sun bore down on the hospital. No air conditioning in those days. The nurse wiped my mother's brow.

My mother Rosa and father Carl

My mother, Rose Wendes, looked out the window at Lake Michigan in the distance, and thanked the Lord that the birth was over with. I was my mother's second child, another boy, since she had left her homeland in Germany and immigrated to the United States in 1927. My father, Carl Wendes (also an immigrant from Germany who came earlier, in 1923) looked at me, a nine-pound baby. He wondered if I was also suffering from the heat. I'm pretty sure I was.

I can faintly recall, if that's possible, that my mother cuddled me in her arms and said, "Ach, mein wunderbare baby, Charles." My father stood by admiring my mother and me.

A little while later a distant relative of my parents, a little bit of a braggart named Charlie, came to visit my mother in the hospital. He asked, "How is Charlie?"

"Nein, nein," my mother retorted, "die name ist Charles, nicht Charlie!"

"Yah, yah, he is Charlie, just like me. Everyone who is Charles in America is called Charlie. That's his nickname."

"Vas? I vas not tinking about nicknames," my mother protested indignantly.

After Uncle Charlie chatted for a while and dropped his little bomb on my mother, he left. My father noted a frown on my mother's face, and that she looked to be in serious thought. "Carl," she proclaimed to my father, "I vant to call our new baby by his middle name, Herbert, instead of Charles. I don't vant people calling him Charlie. Nein, nein, nein!"

"Mein Gott," my father exclaimed. "They already have paperwork done with Charles on it, certificates and other things. I don't think they will allow us to change them."

But my mother was adamant, and they went ahead and called me Herbert instead of Charles thereafter.

My first name was never officially changed from Charles to Herbert. As a consequence, I entered society under false pretenses and had to explain endlessly while growing up—to school personnel, employers, the military service, and so on—why they should call me Herbert instead of Charles, as written on my birth certificate and other official papers.

Chapter 2

A SOUR IMAGE DEVELOPS AS A PRETEEN IN THE 1930s

Some of the branches sprouting out from my tree of life in my youth suffered and wilted along the way. There were some factors that led to the sour image my brothers and parents had of me, which made me feel persecuted and inferior.

I was the only brother who got kicked out of a Wurlitzer accordion class when I was seven years old in about 1937. My parents enrolled me in an accordion training school with great hopes I could play the songs they enjoyed in Germany. What they didn't know was I didn't have an ear for melody and no sense of rhythm, and they were wasting their hard-earned money on my musical culture development.

It was getting close to Christmas and the teacher at Wurlitzer had been trying to get me to play a recognizable rendition of "Silent Night, Holy Night" without much success. My mother thought I was doing fine. One day a friend of my parents, Hilda, visited us and my mother proudly asked if she wanted to hear me play the accordion. So, what German doesn't want to hear an accordion played, even if it's by a seven-year-old who can barely hold up a child-sized model, much less squeeze it back and forth? After I was done with a jerky, goofed-up rendition of "Silent Night," the friend asked, "Rosa, what song was that?" My mother was crestfallen.

After three months of classes, Wurlitzer told us they would give me a medal of completion if I didn't come back.

I was the only brother who had severely crooked and uneven teeth. Some problems in my mouth caused my teeth to grow in very crooked in my early childhood. It happened when getting my second set, after the baby teeth fell out. Because of this I had to wear ugly-

3

looking braces for over four years as a teenager in the later 1940s. I had to take a Chicago streetcar to a dentist on the south side of Chicago from where we lived on the north side (because he was the cheapest guy in town), which took over an hour, twice a week after school. There was an hour or two wait to see the dentist because of shortages of dentists at that time. When I finally was in the dental chair, it only took the dentist 50 seconds to look at my teeth and adjust the tightness on the braces. But after that he would make me sit in the chair for 20 or 30 minutes longer while he took a break, went for a smoke, got a cup of coffee, or took a nap in the storage room.

Then the glorious day came when the braces came off, and I thought I would have a Hollywood smile. I was greatly disappointed. Some teeth were only slightly less crooked than they had been. The upper front teeth, which had a thin bottom edge, were accidentally chipped off in rough-house activities with my brothers and they still looked jagged. It wasn't until later years in the Navy that a dentist asked why I was living with jagged front top teeth and if I wanted to do something about them. I told him I certainly would. He ground the thin bottom edges down and made them a little more even, and my appearance was improved. Many years later, I finally made them look more natural and attractive yet with crowns. You would be surprised at the different reactions you get from people if you have attractive teeth and don't look like you are the Hunchback of Notre Dame.

I was the only brother who got hit by a car on a scooter, racing at breakneck speed down a Chicago alley—another factor in my sour image. I was trying to beat the world's record on a balloon-tired scooter. I was nine years old at the time in 1940, and was pumping ever faster with my right leg. At the end of the alley I began a turn out onto a street, and was looking down, not ahead of me. The car that hit me was turning into the alley. Neither of us saw each other soon enough, because a garage blocked our view, and neither of us slowed down to see what was coming.

We smashed head-on into each other. The couple driving the car said I flew about 20 feet into the air before landing on the concrete alley. I lay on the concrete dazed for a while. The older couple ran from their car to where I was.

"Are you okay? Do you feel pain somewhere? Can you move?"

I wondered if I was okay. I was trying to come to my senses and sort it out. It suddenly popped into my mind that I had been hit by a car. I saw my beloved balloon-tire scooter lying mangled in front of the car. I got up. I was able to stand, but was a little wobbly. The last thing in the world I wanted to do was answer the old couple's questions. I sensed that I didn't have any broken bones. I said, "Yah, I'm okay, I'm okay."

"Are you sure? Should we take you to a doctor?"

"No, no. I'm going to walk home."

The old woman said to her husband, "We had better drive him home and let his mother know what happened." And then she turned to me and said, "We will drive you home."

"Why? I'm okay." But I was disoriented and didn't know which way to go. I wanted to shake them loose. The husband put the mangled scooter in the trunk and the woman took me by the hand and led me to their car.

"We are taking you home! Where do you live?"

"Just down the block on Berteau, 2458."

They explained to my mother, who listened in horror and disbelief about what happened. The couple said they could take me and my mother to a doctor to check me out. I kept on saying, "I'm okay," and they finally left. My mother said I should lie down for a while, which I did. Then I got dizzy and vomited. My mother was horrified.

"Mein Gott, vee are going to the doctor." She called my father at work and told him about it. He said to call a cab and go to our family doctor. We went and I was examined. There were no broken bones, but I was in a little state of shock. He said I might have a mild concussion and told my mother to keep me awake for the rest of the day. Take two aspirin. I got through the night, and the next day I felt better again. However, I cringed at the wrecked mess of my scooter when I looked at it.

When my brothers heard what happened, they nodded and said, "Yah, that's Herb." And my sour image was reinforced.

That is how things were handled in the 1940s. Most people wouldn't dream of fleeing the scene of an accident, a hit and run response. There was no 911 number to call, not many ambulances around, and a scarcity of police. Also, believe it or not, there weren't many attorneys and way fewer lawsuits. People in general were just plain more responsible and trustworthy. And my parents were just happy I was alive and not injured. They would never dream of pressing charges against anyone or filing a greedy lawsuit.

The episodes that gave me a sour image with my family went on. I was the only one who had a fight in the schoolyard when I was about 12 years old. I still had bleached white hair then.

It happened during recess on the school playground—a large area with a full variety of equipment, slides, swings, a Maypole, a merry-go-round, and rings to swing on. There were parallel and single horizontal bars, and more. It was at one end of the school grounds, which covered a full city block. In the middle of the school grounds were two baseball fields used for 16-inch softball and goalposts for football. This area was also used as an ice skating pond in the winter. A three-story brick school building was on the other end, a Chicago public elementary school, kindergarten through eighth grade. The sign on top read *Waters*. A black wrought iron fence wound around the entire block.

During this recess I went over to the horizontal bar in the playground area. A grumpy student, who was in my class, was standing by the bar. He taunted me, "Hey, whitey, who painted your hair white?"

I was taken aback and cringed a bit, but I didn't say anything. I started swinging back and forth on the bar, and deliberately swung my legs widely and kicked him on the arm, but not very hard. I continued swinging, ignoring him as if nothing happened. I didn't say a word.

He got ticked off. "You jerk...watch what you're doing. You looking for a punch in the nose?" He was a short, hefty guy who thought he was superior and tough. In class he acted smugly and I never saw him smile. He swung his arm and hit me in the stomach. I almost lost my grip on the bar, which could have made me fall on the ground and be injured.

I retorted back, "Look out, you moron...you better watch out or you'll be spitting teeth out."

Other classmates heard the threats and gathered around.

"Shut up, you little runt, or I'll push your face in the dirt and make you eat it."

I didn't know what to think of this guy, and couldn't understand why he was so belligerent. I wondered what I was getting into. "Oh yeah?" I retorted again. "Say anything more and you're going to get a bloody nose."

"Aw, shut up you white-haired monkey!"

Friends of mine urged me on.

"You don't have to take that, Herb. Don't put up with his bullying you. Teach him a lesson. Punch him."

We both had gone too far to retreat in front of the other kids watching and didn't want to lose face, so he pushed me and I pushed him back. We started swinging at each other, but got entangled wrestling, which I preferred over getting socked in the face. We went through a humiliating bout of wrestling, boxing, scuffling, sweating and rolling around on the dusty playground—for apparently no good reason.

Our clothes got wrinkled, torn, dirty, and we both got tired of the stalemate. In the end nobody was winning, nor won the fight. The crowd got bored— there was no excitement, no bloody noses, nobody got hurt or knocked out.

"Aw, why don't you two nuts make up and shake hands?" a student yelled out.

7

Wow, was I happy to hear that and I think my opponent was, too. We separated and smiled sheepishly at each other. I think we were both reluctant to shake hands, but we both wanted to put an end to the fight and to look like good guys, so we did. We were also saved by the recess bell, which sounded like a foghorn and summoned us back to the classroom.

As we were walking away from the playground to go back to class, a good friend of mine said to me, "Good fight, Herb…I would never have the guts to do what you did."

I walked on, feeling a little taller.

My brothers heard about the fight, and again said, "That's Herb, always getting into some kind of dumb trouble."

Another incident occurred in the same schoolyard where I had participated in the skirmish. In this case, I was the only brother who fell on his head while leaping from atop a fence to swing on a tree branch. I guess I was watching too many Tarzan movies in the early 1940s. The black wrought iron fence had square bars spaced about six inches apart. They were held together with horizontal bars near the top and bottom and there was enough space between the vertical bars at the top to stand on.

The branch was a little farther away than I thought—almost out of reach. I bent my knees, and stared at the branch, ready to make my leap. I was afraid I might not make it and wondered if I should take the chance. I pushed those thoughts out of my mind for fear I would chicken out; however, I was too excited to turn around, and quickly sprang off the fence toward the branch. I flew through the air and I found I could barely grasp the branch with my fingertips. I had enough of a grip to do half of a gymnastic, giant swing—but not good enough to swing all the way around.

While revolving around the branch in an upside down position in the swing, I lost momentum and my grip. My hold on the branch slipped off, and I plummeted straight down, crashing on the hard earth head first. I was stunned and maybe momentarily lost consciousness. There was no one around to witness my disaster. I regained consciousness, and lay there a little while and inspected the severe bruises on my head and face. I wondered if I might have suffered a concussion. I moved my head and neck back and forth, wiggled my feet, and moved my arms a bit. It didn't seem I had any broken bones and there was no apparent blood gushing out anywhere. Luckily, I didn't break my neck.

Taunts about my bleached white hair came from adults, too, but this one was more my fault. There was a meeting in the assembly hall of Waters Grammar School near the end of the school year. I was nine years old and in the fourth grade. All the students, teachers, and parents in the PTA (Parent-Teacher Association) were seated. Some dignitaries from the Chicago Public Schools system sat in the back, making observations about the school.

The principal of the school, who had grey hair and fastidious and prudish manners, was standing in front of the audience giving a speech. Between each momentous remark, she paused, smiled from ear to ear, and stared intently at the school dignitaries and parents. There was a little squeak in her falsetto voice as she bragged about how wonderful her school was. She was sure she had impressed the audience.

I sat along the middle aisle and watched the principal walk back and forth as she spoke. I had gotten bored with her talk and with the artificiality of it. In the middle of one segment, talking about how to efficiently look up words in a dictionary, she instructed, "Start by opening up the dictionary in the approximate area of where the word might be. For example, if the word starts with a *C*, open up near the front of the book; if an *L*, near the center; and with a *V*, near the back..." Just as she was about to finish that sentence I stretched my arms out and let out a loud yawn, which resonated all over the auditorium. She was near to where I was sitting and could see me perfectly. She stopped her dissertation and in the next breath said in a haughty tone, "If that towhead would listen more he certainly could learn something."

I didn't know what "towhead" meant at that time, so I wasn't bothered by her remark, and I didn't pay any attention to the people seated around me, who I heard were a little shocked and uncomfortable.

Later on, some of my friends asked me if I was embarrassed in the assembly hall when the principal spoke. "Over what?" I asked them.

"Over the principal calling you a towhead."

"Why, what does that mean?" I asked.

"It means someone with white hair, you dope."

"She had a lot of nerve," I defended myself. "I was tired, that's why I yawned." I started to worry I might be in trouble, but nothing ever happened. However, I avoided bumping into the principal in school for the rest of my grammar school days.

The principal was wrong about me. I was listening, because from that day on whenever I have looked up a word in a dictionary, I have done so exactly as she instructed.

Another Herb accident happened while waiting on customers in my parents' delicatessen. At various times when my parents were very busy in the store, my older brother and I had to help out waiting on customers. The store was mobbed on this Saturday afternoon in 1946.

I cut my thumb slicing bologna while waiting on customers in my family's delicatessen.

10

I was cutting baloney on the slicing machine behind the deli counter. The deli refrigerator was filled with German and American cold cuts, such as sausages, liver sausage, ham, Jagdwurst, salami, and more. Much of it was from specialty German sausage companies like Kochs, Koenemens, and Unsingers from Milwaukee, and American Oscar Mayer. Fresh German and American potato salads, which my mother made, were in bowls.

People were waiting impatiently to order and my brother and mother were in line behind me waiting to use the slicing machine. The pressure made me nervous and I started to cut the baloney faster. My hand slipped and the blade cut into the skin of my thumb. Rudy was right behind me, and when he saw what happened he took the pile of baloney with spots of blood on it and threw it into the garbage. Thankfully, I don't think the customers noticed what happened.

I ran into the kitchen in back of the store and let cold water run over the cut. I saw the flap hanging there on my thumb and flipped it over on top of the cut. "The bleeding ain't slowing down," I told my brother, who had followed me into the kitchen. "Tell Pa! Get him in here, now." There was fear in my voice. Rudy told my father what had happened and that the cut thumb wouldn't stop bleeding.

My father, irritated that he was being interrupted with a store full of customers, excused himself. "Pardon me for a minute...there is a little emergency...I'll be right back," he said, and came into the kitchen. He saw the cut and blood oozing out. "Du dummkopf," he said. He was always saying that to us kids. He grabbed a cup and filled it with flour. He told me, "Stick your thumb into the flour and leave it there until the bleeding stops," then he went right back out into the store to tend to the customers.

After a while the bleeding slowed down a little, but not enough. My brother, who had gone back out into the store also, came back in and asked, "How is it going?"

"Not so good...what should I do?" I answered.

He looked at the reddened flour in the cup. "Umm...use another cup of fresh flour...here, I'll get it for you."

I stuck my thumb in the second cup of flour, praying it would stop the bleeding. After a spell the bleeding slowed down and almost stopped.

My father came back in to check on me. "How is the bleeding?" he asked.

"Better," I said.

My father inspected the flour in the cup, which was only tinted red, and said that was enough. He brushed the flour off the cut and dabbed some iodine on it, which really stung. He flipped the flap, which was still hanging on the thumb, back where it belonged over the cut, then put a thick pad of gauze on the cut and wrapped medical tape tightly around the gauze and thumb. The bleeding finally stopped.

Later, my mother worried that the cut might need stitches, and took me to our doctor, Dr. Ansdorf, an older German gentleman. He didn't think it required stitching. He cleaned the wound, put some antiseptic on it, rebandaged it and told us to keep it well bandaged for a couple of days. He then asked me, "By the way, when did you have your last tetanus shot?" I couldn't remember ever having one so he proceeded to jab a needle into my arm, which I wasn't too happy about.

My father's help with the cup of flour saved the day for me, along with my brother's quick action and my mother's caution in taking me to the doctor. I don't think I ever showed how I appreciated what they did. However, later at home my brother smugly criticized me by saying, "Why can't you watch what you are doing, you dope?"

"Watch out what you are saying or I'll stick your nose in the slicing machine," I snapped back in my most nasty way.

I was the only brother that caught a contagious scalp infection, ringworm, when I was in grammar school. I had to wear a nylon stocking on my head to prevent spreading it—a big embarrassment. That year, about 1943, there was an epidemic developing in the school and some other kids caught it, too. But most of them either didn't go to school until they were better, or just didn't wear the nylon stocking in school. Nylon hosiery was scarce during the war because they needed the nylon for parachutes, so I figured why should I take one of my mother's few pairs to wear on my head?

Of course, my brothers Rudy and Paul, who were going to the same grade school, didn't become infected with ringworm. I sank further down the image totem pole in their eyes, even though it was through no fault of my own.

Bottom line on my sour image with the family: I didn't have much control over the conditions and incidents I was faced with as a child. I was a little kid, a short guy with white hair, crooked teeth, a weak bladder, a feeling of inferiority, and more. Other times kids teased me, "You little shrimp!" "Hey shorty!" "When are you going to grow up, midget?" "Hey, little guy!"

All this, plus more, convinced me that there was something wrong with me. Consequently, I started blushing easily. Then I developed an intense fear of blushing when talking to someone, or if I just thought they were looking at me. And when I felt that I was starting to blush, whether I was or not, the fear panicked me, and sure enough the resultant anxiety produced redness in my face; this caused excessive anxiety and made me lose confidence in myself.

Chapter 3
MISCHIEVOUS SHENANIGANS

Teenage Years in the 1940s

As a teenager in the 1940s, I was almost a juvenile delinquent...but I never quite made it. Adolescents and teenage boys back then were involved in many mischievous pranks. I would like to say it was almost required to maintain a macho image. Even though I wasn't the only brother involved in these shenanigans, I overdid my share of them.

Shooting Out Streetlamps

One of the shenanigans, which I committed a couple of times for excitement, was to shoot out the streetlight in front of our bungalow house on the north side in Chicago. My older brother and I slept in the attic bedroom, which had a double window facing the street. There was a streetlamp in front of our house on the right side.

Bungalow house we lived in on Berteau in Chicago,
where I shot out a streetlamp with my BB gun and
snuck out of the house from the attic window.

One evening I was alone in our attic bedroom. My parents were working in the delicatessen, and my brother was out. I got the impulse to get my BB gun and see if I could hit the streetlamp. I loaded the BBs into the rifle, turned the bedroom lights off so no one could see me, and opened the window a little. I pumped up the gun, stuck the barrel through the window opening, and aimed at the streetlamp. I got a bead on the lamp and aimed a little higher (because the BBs tended to fall a bit with distance), and pulled the trigger. The BB missed the lamp and hit the metal post below, making a cast iron *ping*. I readjusted the height above the light to compensate for the drop. This time the BB pinged on the bulb. My mouth fell opened as the lamp exploded, gas hissed out loudly, and the light faded away.

I looked around the street to see if anyone was around, and worried I might get caught. I moved away from the window, stored the gun away in the corner of a closet, then went downstairs and pretended to be reading when my parents and brother came home. For the next several weeks I envisioned that the police and Commonwealth Edison would investigate and would catch me, and put me in reform school. Fortunately, it never happened.

Sneaking Out of the House When Grounded

The same bedroom window was also used for sneaking out of the house when I was grounded by my mother. One evening, as I sat in my bedroom around seven o'clock after dinner—despondent, bored, and lonely from being grounded—I heard my friend, Dave, calling me from in front of the house.

"Yaohh, Herb, yaohh Herb!"

This is the way you let your friends know you were there in those days. You didn't go to the front or back door and disturb the whole house by knocking on the door or ringing the bell.

I perked up and opened the window so I could stick my head through it. "Hi, Dave. I'm up here in my bedroom."

Dave was a personable, sociable, friendly and articulate guy who had moved to Chicago from Wisconsin when he was about eight or nine years old. We became friends right away because my parents had friends who owned a farm in the same town Dave came from, Kiel, and I had been out there a number of times. We could both relate to Kiel.

"How about coming out and we can go to Harry's."

It was an ice cream parlor and magazine store with a pinball machine where you could win a chocolate milkshake. We hung out with other friends, Frank, Bill, Larry, Herb and other neighborhood guys. It was the local meeting place a couple of blocks away from my house, and had mom and pop owners, Harry and Grace. They were friendly and let us hang around, even when we didn't buy anything.

"I can't go, I'm grounded tonight," I whined.

"Aw, can't you talk to your mother and see if she will change her mind?"

Being grounded was not the usual thing with my parents. Both Dave and I were disappointed and didn't like the idea of being suppressed with a grounding.

"Naw, I don't think she will change her mind. She doesn't sound like she is in the mood."

"Maybe you could sneak out some way and slip back in without her knowing."

I got excited about the idea of being able to sneak out. I looked around the porch roof below me, which extended out about 10 feet. Posts on both corners of the roof held it up on the front end. My house was very close to the two-story brick apartment house next door on the right side. There was only about a foot and a half of space between the two houses.

"Maybe I can climb down the post on the right side without anybody seeing me and squeeze in between the two houses."

"Yah, that's an idea, but don't forget you'll have to climb up again to get back in the house without anybody knowing it," Dave cautioned.

"I think I can do it. Wait a minute while I get ready. Come up on the porch, Dave...quietly...and maybe you can help me guide my feet onto the banister when I slide down the post."

"Okay. I'll be right under you."

I climbed out on the roof and figured out how to position myself so I could slide down the corner post. Dave guided my feet to the banister and I eased my way down to the porch floor. We tiptoed down the stairs of the porch and spent the next two hours at Harry's Confectionary and Ice Cream Store goofing around with the gang, then I decided to get back a little early just in case my mother was checking on me.

On the way back we thought it would be fun if Dave stayed overnight at my house. We stopped at his house on the way back from Harry's and Dave asked his mother if it was okay if he slept overnight at my house. No problem. She knew me well and enough about my family to give permission.

When we got back to the house we reversed the process, going up. I went up the pole and onto the roof first, and then Dave followed me up. Kneeling on the porch roof, I opened the window and we both crawled into the bedroom.

I was nervous that my mother had found out that I had snuck out, so I called down the stairway, "Hey, Mom, can I get something to eat? I'm hungry."

She came to the stairway. "Yaah, you been a good boy and suffered enough."

I was happy she hadn't checked on me while I was gone. She was probably happy things were quiet and peaceful.

I went downstairs and made a couple of sandwiches, one for myself and the other for Dave, and brought them upstairs along with some pop. We ate them, excited about getting away with something. Much later, after talking and talking, we slept soundly.

The next morning we woke up early and Dave tiptoed down the stairs, snuck by my younger brother, who happened to be up, and went out the back door before my parents were up. They didn't hear anything and they never found out about the escapade.

Halloween Pranks

On Halloween, tradition made us, so we thought, dump over garbage cans in the Chicago alleys, and maybe even tear down a fence if it looked old and rickety enough.

Another favorite Halloween prank was to go into an apartment building's entrance, press many of the doorbells, and stick pins alongside the buttons, which would keep the button depressed and buzzing until the people came down to the entrance and removed the pin. People would holler down through the voice tubes to the mail boxes, "Who is there?" "Stop ringing!" "Are you guys nuts!" We ran off as fast as we could right after they responded.

On Halloween, boys also believed it was their duty to put stink bombs by people's front doors. Old photo film was wrapped in newspapers and twisted around on each end. You would sneak up the porch stairs of a house, light one end of the newspaper and press the door bell several times quickly—to make it sound like an emergency. By the time the people came to the door and opened it to look out, the film inside the newspaper was burning and created an insidious stink. The people would see the smoke and flames and stamp it out with their feet, and shout some choice curses.

The old red streetcars of this era in Chicago had an open platform in the back where people stepped up and boarded. A conductor stood on the platform next to the door leading to the inside seating area to collect fares. There were usually a few people in the boarding area, either waiting to pay or because they didn't want to go into the seating area. It was easier to hop off at your stop from the back platform than to go out the front door of the streetcar.

One time on Halloween we threw eggs in back of a red streetcar on Western Avenue as it went by—a sorry prank indeed, but we thought it was exciting. The eggs splattered on the loading platform, on the people standing there, and on the conductor. The conductor pulled the emergency stop cord on the streetcar, jumped out on the street (much to our surprise and fear) and started chasing us as if he was going to murder us. We ran down a side street and disappeared between the houses and alleys.

When Smoking Was Fashionable

My older brother participated in some of the same shenanigans that I did as an adolescent. We both smoked cigarettes when we were 15 or 16 years old. It was fashionable in those days and adults all over the place were smoking. Hollywood and advertisements glorified and glamorized it. Tobacco companies handed out small packages of cigarettes to students and military men to get them started on smoking. Even my younger brother, Paul, indulged in smoking.

Norb and I were "in fashion" smoking as teenagers.

Teenagers could buy cigarettes pretty much at that time. When I sold them in our delicatessen they were only 21 cents for a package of 20. Camels, Lucky Strikes, Pall Malls, and Chesterfields were some of the popular brands in the 1940s, which helped people get lung cancer in later years. The only filter cigarette that was available in the 1940s I believe were Kools.

Your teeth and fingers would get yellow nicotine stains on them. You breathed deeply to inhale the smoke into your lungs. You would impress people by inhaling and by blowing out smoke circles. Particles of ash in the smoke would often go up your nostrils and make you gag.

We believed, in those days, it was hip and okay to smoke. We felt this was the life we must lead in order to be happy. Boys stood on corners or in front of small restaurants across the street from Chicago high schools with cigarettes dangling out of their mouths. These were the real hotshots of our day, Hollywood style.

I can't remember that there were any reports on the bad effects of smoking on your health at that time. We were innocent. The big bombs of the terrible effects of smoking and nicotine started to hit the streets in the 1950s. In 1947, at the age of 16, I was smoking a pack a day.

In 1955 when I was 24 years old and in the Navy, I was smoking heavily, about 30 cigarettes a day. Although it was an era where it was popular to smoke, I decided to give it up and I did. My fingers were stained with nicotine. I would be brushing my teeth in the morning and taking drags on a cigarette off and on as I brushed and rinsed my mouth. The cigarette would dangle from my mouth as I shaved with my electric shaver and the smoke would go up my nose and I would gag. I coughed from the smoking and food didn't taste as good anymore. The last thing I did before I went to sleep at night was smoke a cigarette. I had to constantly see that I had a package of cigarettes with me, as well as matches or a lighter. I had to have an ashtray around when inside.

"That is it," I told myself. I just happened to read the *Reader's Digest Magazine's* condensation of a book at that time of *How to Quit Smoking*, a step-by-step psychological method of stopping. It was full of practical techniques for how to break old, bad habits and replace them with new, good habits by applying some self-hypnotism and affirmations, plus positive thinking. I went to sleep at night saying to myself, *Tomorrow I won't smoke, tomorrow I won't smoke.* When I got up in the morning I said to myself, *This day I will not smoke, this day I will not smoke.*

I didn't swear to myself *I'm going to quit smoking forever,* which has the tendency to overwhelm you, and weaken your confidence in being able to quit. Instead, I approached each urge to smoke a cigarette one at a time. I told myself, *Every time I overcome the urge to smoke, I am becoming stronger and stronger.* The book urged you to keep telling yourself of the huge benefits of not smoking; of avoiding potential lung diseases; of smoker's cough; of the costs, hassles and nuisance of the bad habit.

The techniques go on like that in the book, and if followed faithfully, they work. They did with me and I haven't smoked for over 50 years.

When Drinking Beer Was Popular, But Not Fashionable

Beer was popular but not as fashionable as smoking in the 1930s, '40s and '50s.

Not only did my older brother and I smoke cigarettes when we were about 15 or 16 years old (young), but we also began to drink beer about the same time. In the German-Irish neighborhood I lived in, older children could go to the local tavern and drink beer, like on a Friday night, and have a grand old time. Also, if you went into a restaurant with your parents you could usually get a beer with your meal even if you were a teenager. Many families let older teenagers drink beer at the dinner table or in home parties.

However, what the parents didn't know is that we also would sit in somebody's car in the alley at times and drink half-gallon bottles of beer, which were popular in those days. Usually when I drank the half-gallon bottle I got sick before I finished it. And again, my younger brother Paul didn't follow in his two older brothers' footsteps. He didn't sit in a car in the alley and drink beer; or at least, I never knew that he did.

To buy the beer when we were so young meant you had to have

either a fake or altered identity card, which in those days were draft cards showing your age. We knew a guy who worked in a print shop. "Herb," he said, "I can print you a fake card, an exact replica of the real one, for five dollars. Then all you have to do is sign it and you will be in business."

The alternative to buying a printed card, which wouldn't cost me anything, was to erase the year of birth on the real card with an ink eraser and then fudge in the year that made you old enough to drink beer legally. In those days, five dollars to me was like a hundred dollars today. I declined. "Naw, five bucks is too much for me, I'll just change the birth date on my card," I told him. You could also buy a stolen draft card for five dollars.

When I was getting together with my neighborhood buddies for a beer session, and it was my turn to buy the beer, I would go to a liquor store to buy it. Sometimes they didn't card me and other times they did. When they asked to see my ID they usually accepted my altered card, and didn't say anything. Apparently, they didn't care whether I was too young or not, even if it was obvious. I think some of the stores paid off the cops and others just took a chance because they didn't want to lose the sales.

So, I became confident at being able to buy beer illegally. I felt that it was my *right* to do so and the laws were wrong. But one time when trying to buy beer, I was shocked at what happened! I found out that I had to be better prepared to avoid getting tripped up. It nearly ended my days of buying beer. I was 15 years old when the beer buying started in 1946. To make me old enough to buy beer I had to change the birth date on the card from 1931 to, I think, 1925.

Then one day when trying to buy beer at a liquor store, the salesclerk asked to see my identification card and things got hot. I fished it out of my wallet and gave it to him. He stared at it for a minute. For me it seemed like 10 minutes. He looked back and forth between the date on the card and my face. I got red and nervous. He looked me straight in the eye and asked, "When were you born?"

I couldn't think of the right year to make me old enough. My mind froze. I got nervous and stammered, "Er, uh..." My mind fumbled with the math and got all jumbled up. I think even if I had remembered it, I would have been afraid to say it. Lying wasn't my best suit. I looked down at the floor and quietly said, "On second thought, I better recheck what my parents wanted before I buy anything," and I started to scamper out of the store.

"Hey, wait a minute!" the clerk yelled. He walked toward me. I got scared and almost started to run. He said, "Here, take your ID card with you."

One of my friends in the beer drinking group, Norb, was a taller, huskier guy, who looked much older. Generally, the stores sold him beer without questioning his age. We let him buy the beer after my embarrassing episode in the liquor store. As the World War II years faded away, the loose control started to change. They beefed up the laws and started clamping down on sales to minors. Many people grumbled about it and thought it was outrageous.

But unlike smoking, which lost its fashionability over the years, drinking beer is not only more popular yet, but has also become more fashionable. Television, advertising, light beer, micro breweries, imports and convenient containers have made it a frontrunner in social drinking. It has replaced drinking champagne, which was once the height of fashionability. Champagne is now scoffed at by most of the mainstream public today, except for toasting on special occasions.

Graduating From Beer to Booze

When we were about 17 or 18 years old, we wanted to graduate from beer drinking to some stronger alcohols. It was New Year's Eve and the guys in our group, who hung around together, decided to celebrate. My friend Herb, who lived across the street from me, says he was the one who got hold of a fifth of some whiskey, but I think it was our older-looking, beer-buying guy Norb who bought it.

We had no clue about the potency of whiskey, we just wanted to celebrate and experiment with something we weren't familiar with.

We reasoned, our parents drank whiskey at times, why can't we?

We walked down Chicago neighborhood streets on our way to Marianne's house, who had invited us to come over to celebrate New Year's Eve. Marianne was one of the friends in the group and we went to school together.

As we walked we kept taking swigs right out of the bottle openly on the streets. "Hey, give me the bottle, I'm next." We took a couple of swigs and didn't feel anything, so we assumed that the alcohol wasn't that bad. "It's my turn again!" And we took a bunch more swigs in a hurry and found we still were reasonably okay, then some more. *When is this stuff going to work?* I thought. Then I found out. Just as we arrived at Marianne's house, *wham!* We got hit and were in another world, which we didn't know much about.

I don't remember and wasn't aware of what happened at the girl's house, nor, for that matter, what happened for the next few hours. "What happened when we reached Marianne's? Did we go in? Did we even get there?" I asked a couple of the guys, who didn't participate in the whiskey drinking. They told us: "A bunch of guys who drank the bottle of whiskey got to the girl's house and raised a ruckus there. You then left and were escorted back to where you live by us sober Good Samaritans. If we hadn't done that you would be lying in a gutter somewhere."

Not only was there some barfing on the streets as we walked back, there was barfing all over the place in my living room. My friend Herb tried to hide the smell of the barf by spraying perfume all over the place. We slowly passed out. My sober friends put me to bed and covered me with a mountain of blankets because I was shivering.

Herb went across the street to his house and tried to sneak up the stairs quietly. His father, who had been waiting up for him to come home, heard him stumble up the stairs. He waited at the top of the stairway and confronted him with his hands on his hips. Big trouble.

The other whiskey drinkers disappeared, either because they were dropped off at their houses already on the way back, or got home without a disaster. No one got hit by a car, no one was injured otherwise, nor ended up in jail. Miraculously, we all made it through the night. Upon awakening, we had no idea what had happened.

But then, the storm from my parents hit me. Everybody had left and I was out as though someone had muzzled me with chloroform. The smells of the perfume and alcohol permeated the house. It was early morning, about four or five o'clock. My parents had come back early from a Wisconsin New Year's party instead of staying overnight. My mother shook me vigorously over and over. She couldn't stir me one bit. I was extinguished like a burnt-out match. She didn't know if I was dead or not, but probably wished she could choke me to death at that moment. I couldn't wake up and I muttered like a drunkard. She yelled at me, "What happened? Where were you? Where did you get the whiskey? Why, why, why? Who else was here? I told you not to bring any friends into our house while we were gone. Why didn't you do what I told you?"

When I woke up late the next morning I explained to my parents, "I don't know what happened. The other guys were drinking the whiskey and talked me into trying some, so I sipped a little. I passed out and they brought me and some other guys home." I'm not sure if my parents bought my story, but I stuck to it rigidly.

The following afternoon my friend Herb's father gave us a two-hour lecture about the evils and dangers of whiskey drinking. "You could have died. Too much whiskey can be a poison. I want you two to swear you will never do this again."

"Yes, yes," we swore. "It won't ever happen again."

And it never did happen again. We were lucky to survive without a tragedy and learned our lesson, despite our youthful foolishness of growing up and experimenting through trial and error with dangerous things in life.

The gang hanging out at Marianne's
house when we were about 16 years old.

Shot BB Gun at Outhouse on Farm

For a couple of years, when I was about 15 or 16 years old, in the later 1940s, I went to work on a farm just south of Sheboygan, Wisconsin, near Lake Michigan, for several weeks during the summer. I pitched hay, hooked up the horses to the wagon, brought the cows in for milking, and did other menial chores. The old German couple who ran the 160-acre dairy farm were friends of my parents. They could barely speak English and had rickety, stained teeth. The wife talked with a rasp in her throat that reminded me of Ma and Pa Kettle in the movies, except that half her words were in German instead of English.

She was nice and couldn't do enough to please me; breakfast with homemade bread and strawberry jelly; fresh, real butter that she churned; and fresh, farm fried chicken. For Sunday dinners she would tell her husband to go out to the chicken coop and cut the heads off of a chicken or two. Then she spent an hour or two plucking the feathers out.

However, this episode was not about those good things. Rather, it occurred with another character in the story, the 17-year-old farmer's daughter, Elsie. This isn't a farmer's daughter story. Sorry about that. She was an intelligent, quiet, and plump girl, and kept to herself.

I had gotten a BB gun for my birthday shortly before going out to the farm and was anxious to do some fancy shooting while out there. So, one afternoon when I wasn't busy with farming tasks and was moseying around looking for something to shoot at, I saw Elsie go into the outhouse, which was about a hundred feet behind their house. The walls of the outhouse were made of wood planks, six or eight inches wide, with spacing between them for ventilation and light. I thought hitting the plank right in the middle would be a challenging target, and would give Elsie a scare while she was in the outhouse. After all, she didn't pay much attention to me, anyway. She also would never know what the ping of the BB off the board was— maybe just an animal or insect, so I thought.

I pumped up the BB gun, took careful aim from behind a clump of bushes, and made sure no one was around who could see me. Also, I didn't want the pellet to accidentally go through the cracks and hit Elsie, so I rechecked my aim, held the rifle steady and pulled the trigger. Bang! The sound of the copper BB bouncing off the wood board echoed far across the fields of the farm.

I was glad the BB didn't go through a crack, and thought I was in the clear. But then, much to my surprise, I heard a loud scream, saw the outhouse door fling open, and Elsie racing toward the house, her dress flopping up and down in the wind.

I thought, *Uh-oh...I better not rush into the house or they will suspect me.* So, I hung around outside, out of sight, for an hour or so. The farmer came back from the field later in the afternoon after mowing hay. I ran to him and offered to help him unhook the horses. Then when he went into the house, I snuck in behind him and went right up to my room on the second floor.

At dinnertime I went downstairs, feeling sheepish. We ate dinner and it was strangely quiet. Elsie and her mother kept on frowning and shooting visual daggers at me. Elsie left before she finished dinner, which she never did otherwise. They must have known it was me who had done this misdeed from the guilty look on my face, my squeaky voice at the table…and the fact that I had a new BB gun.

I was glad that my two- or three-week stay was up a few days later, and that my parents would pick me up. The farmer's wife and Elsie weren't all that friendly with my parents, but didn't say anything about me shooting at the outhouse. However, that ended my farm life in Wisconsin. The old couple never asked me to come out to the farm again, even though I was a big help to them and they didn't have to pay me.

And somehow my two brothers got wind of my escapade there, and my image went further down the totem pole with them.

Playing Hooky in High School

Another area of engaging in slightly delinquent behavior was playing hooky from school when attending Lane Tech High School in Chicago around 1947. But I wasn't the only brother who did so. I was following in my older brother's footsteps in this case. Sometimes, as a bunch of my friends and I walked to Lane Tech High School in the morning, on nice spring days with the sun shining, the grass turning green, trees and bushes sprouting leaves after the terrible Chicago winters, someone would say, "I don't feel like going to school today!"

"Yah, I don't either," most of us chimed in.

"Where should we go, downtown to the Chicago Theater?"

Someone mentioned that they heard Mickey Rooney and Judy Garland were there in person. At that time you could see a first-run movie and a live stage show for 25 cents for kids. If that was the plan we agreed on, we would hop on a Chicago elevated train for something like three or four cents, and walk around the Chicago Loop until the show started at the Chicago Theater. No one questioned us as to why we weren't in school and truant officers didn't seem to be around anywhere.

Other ways we spent the day playing hooky: Someone would suggest on these bright sunny days going down to the Wilson Avenue Rocks or Montrose Beach along Lake Michigan. In this case, we took a streetcar to the lake and spent the day there goofing around and eating the brown bag lunches, which our parents made for us, on picnic benches. We were all happy during the day while playing hooky, but not so happy later that evening about having to write fake excuses for being absent. We helped each other forge our parents' signatures on the excuse letters, which we had to take to school the next day.

I think I was influenced a bit by my older brother Rudy, who did his share of cutting school. In my eyes it meant it was okay to do so if your older brother did it.

But he did it right, pretty much getting away with it. He had some of his classmate friends, who attended school and didn't cut, tell him what the homework assignments were and when the tests would be given. He would have his friends hand in his homework and would make sure he attended school on test days. He also wrote forged excuse letters.

But, one time Rudy went too far. The school summer vacation had just ended and his full-time summer job of working in a laundry on the drying machines had to come to an end. He didn't want to lose the money he was making at the laundry and he kept working full-time for the first three weeks of the new semester. After three weeks, the school started to inquire, "Where the heck is this guy?" and it caught up with him. Our stepfather had to go to school and get things straightened out.

Playing Hooky From Confirmation Classes

I didn't limit myself to just cutting school. When I was going to confirmation classes after school on Fridays for about two years, my friend Dave and I would occasionally look at each other and both say at the same time, "I don't feel like going to confirmation today. What do we do, then?"

One of us suggested, "We could go shoot pool at the Lawrence Avenue Bowling Alley."

"Okay, let's go!" And we would walk two blocks further and shoot pool for a couple of hours until it was time to go home for dinner.

We didn't think the pastor cared too much if we were there every session or not, but it was funny how he called on my friend or me after we missed a session to recite the Apostle's Creed, the Lord's Prayer, or maybe the Ten Commandments. We went to the front of the class and fumbled around with the incomplete recitations until we were sufficiently embarrassed in front of our peers, and then he let us sit down. We thought he had a lot of nerve for a person that we thought was really a friendly, nice guy. Ultimately, we learned most of the stuff from Luther's Catechism and the pastor allowed us to graduate and get confirmed.

Those were some of the deeds that we were involved with, which were maybe not as bad as they sound. We knew we were fighting the system, doing something wrong, but we figured if we could get away with it, and it was exciting, and we didn't hurt anybody, it was worth it. Anyway, we were basically good kids with other important values, which we followed. We soon grew up and shed our adolescent ways.

Hitchhiking to the Dells

In the 1940s, after WWII was over, there weren't many cars around in the U.S. The automobile companies, who stopped producing civilian cars during the war, were gearing up to switch from manufacturing military equipment and going back to producing cars again for the public. But it was taking some time. There weren't many commercial airline planes, either. The popular modes of transportation for any distance were buses or trains.

Three of my friends, Dave, Herb, Norb, and myself wanted to go to the Wisconsin Dells, an up-and-coming vacation spot. It was about a 150-mile trip from Chicago, and we didn't want to spend money on bus fares; and since we were all just 17 years old, we couldn't get a car. Hitchhiking was acceptable and reasonably safe then. Some people would usually pick you up along the highway.

We left in the morning on a bright, sunny day in October of 1948, took a streetcar to get to the edge of Chicago where the highways began, and started swinging our thumbs to let cars know we wanted to hitch a ride as they zoomed by. A half an hour went by as we kept walking northward in the direction of the Dells without an offer for a ride. Finally, an old car with a young farmer stopped and he asked, "Where are you going?" We told him the Dells. "I'm not going that far but I could take you guys 20 some miles in that direction."

"That's great. We sure appreciate it."

We all piled into his car and rode the 20 miles. After he let us off, we resumed swinging our thumbs to flag down cars again. A few went by, but no takers stopped for over an hour. We decided there probably weren't many people who would stop for four teenagers, so two of us starting doing the hiking sign and the other two guys hid off the road. A friendly old couple in a 1932 Ford stopped and said, "We are going to the next town, about 30 miles down the road." We told them we had two more friends with us, and would it be okay if they came along? The old couple looked at each other, smiled, and said, "Sure, why not?" We motioned to the two guys hiding behind the bushes to come out. The couple was talkative and friendly. It was a fun ride. We couldn't say thank you enough and they loved it.

Hitchhiking to the Dells in Wisconsin

But we were still over 100 miles away from the Dells. In the next town we did the hitchhiking wave again, but nobody stopped for a couple of hours. Our patience and confidence wore thin. It was mid-afternoon already. At the rate we were going hitchhiking, it looked like it might take the rest of the day and half the night before we got to the Dells, if at all. So, we decided to try and get a Greyhound bus for the rest of the trip. We walked to the next closest town, inquired as to where the Greyhound bus terminal was, and got there somehow. At the Greyhound bus station we went to the ticket window and asked, "We want to go to the Wisconsin Dells. Do you have anything scheduled for today?"

"You guys hit the jackpot. We have a bus leaving for the Dells in a half an hour and we got some empty seats. It should arrive there about seven o'clock this evening. How many tickets do you want?"

Wow! Were we happy. The two-hour bus ride was a relief from

hiking and it was about seven o'clock when we got to the Dells.

But further problems popped up that we never expected in the Dells. We decided the first thing we should do, even before eating dinner somewhere, was find a place we could rent and sleep overnight, maybe get a breakfast with it, too. In the 1940s the Dells wasn't a big vacation spot, there were hardly any motels, and people just rented out rooms in the houses. We looked for rental signs and found one. We explained to the homeowner, "We just got here from Chicago and need a couple of rooms for four people tonight."

"Sorry, we are filled up tonight, but we can give you an address of another place that may have something."

"Great. Could you give us directions to get there?"

They explained how to get there, but they only had one small room available with one single bed. We went hunting again and the next couple of places were either full or didn't have adequate accommodations. It was dark, getting later in the evening, and we were hungry, so we stopped to eat.

We finished eating and left the restaurant and were about to start to search again for a room when an attractive girl—with slightly red hair, an innocent, cute, and fresh Wisconsin farm look about her, about our age—came into the restaurant. All four of us stared wide-eyed at her. She saw us in the restaurant too, and was curious where we were from. She said hi and gave us a smile. We hi'd her back. We told her we were there from Chicago for the weekend and of our sleeping plight. She offered, "I might be able to help you out. I know of a couple of places that rent out rooms. I can show you where they are if you want."

"Yah, would you...that would be nice," we all chimed in. As we walked to the first place we got into a friendly conversation with her and we were glad to have a friend helping us. We chatted as we went to the two places she knew of, but neither could handle four guys. Then she said, "It's late and I have to go home. I hope you guys find something."

"Goodbye, thank you for your help, thank you!" we all exclaimed.

"Now what?" we asked each other. "There is a park that we passed a block down. Maybe we can find something to sleep on there."

We walked to the park. The grass was wet with dew and the benches too narrow and hard. It was getting to be a cold fall night and we were shivering, bewildered, and worn out. Someone suggested, "Maybe we can find some way to sleep in the park toilet building," which was a nice-sized brick structure. We inspected the inside of it and decided to fashion some way to sleep, using rolls of toilet paper for pillows and newspaper for sheets on the cold concrete floor. After a half an hour of lying on the cold, hard concrete floor, no one slept and we decided it was no use trying anymore. We went out to the streets again and wondered what the heck we were going to do; should we walk around all night and try to catch a bus back home in the morning? What a disastrous failure our hitchhiking trip would end up being—without even seeing the beauty of the Dells.

We figured if we knocked on any more doors at 11 o'clock in the evening and people peeked through their windows and saw four teenage boys standing there, they wouldn't even open the door, much less rent us a room. We kept wandering around, not really knowing which way to go, and passed one of the houses we had checked with earlier. Suddenly, a woman we talked to before opened her front door quickly and yelled at us, "Hey boys...boys, come here a minute!"

We were a bit leery about what was going on and we walked slowly to her front door. "I told a friend of mine who rents rooms about you four nice boys not being able to find a place to sleep...and she says she has a big bedroom with a king-size bed...and if you don't mind sleeping in it a bit cramped...you are welcome to it."

"Yes, ma'am, we don't mind. We'll sleep on a bed of nails if we have to."

We went to the woman's house and all four of us slept crossways on the bed, and got up about nine in the morning. She offered us a nice big breakfast for a dollar each. We took her up on it, gobbled up fresh Wisconsin eggs, bacon, toast with rich Wisconsin butter, pancakes, French toast, and whatever else there was. We paid her for the room and breakfast and thanked her for the wonderful treatment.

We had just left her house and started to get information on sightseeing in the Dells when a police car stopped us and interrogated us. "Where are you guys from? When did you get into town? Why were you roaming around the streets at night and in the park?" They didn't like the idea too much that we were from Chicago. We were scared, but we answered all the questions honestly, exactly as it was. They called the restaurant, the woman whose house we had stayed at, the Greyhound bus terminal, and even the girl that helped us out. Everything checked out and the police began to ease up on us. We were in the dark as to why we were being grilled and they finally told us that a Ford Model T had been stolen during the night and they had suspected that we might be the culprits.

That was enough excitement for us all, so we just did some sightseeing during the day, and took a boat tour through the Dells. We boarded a bus early in the evening that took us back to Chicago.

We got home, bragged about our adventures, and were happy to sleep peacefully and securely in our own comfortable beds.

Chapter 4
GOOD TWIGS START TO GROW

After all the goofy and somewhat irresponsible activities I participated in during my adolescent years, one might conclude I really was a full-fledged juvenile delinquent. But as I said before, I never quite made it. Fortunately, there were mitigating circumstances, and some positive behavior while I was growing up, which one could ascribe to my German genes. Who knows?

I was an enthusiastic amateur photographer. One positive episode was when I joined the camera club in high school during my sophomore year in 1950. A dozen or so students turned up after school for the first meeting, where we decided to have a photography contest. I was then, and still am, an avid photographer, so I rummaged through photos I had taken in the past.

We were allowed to make three entries in the contest. I chose what I thought were my best black-and-white pictures. One was of my younger brother Paul and his friend sitting on a snow sled late in fall with disgruntled expressions on their faces due to the fact there was no snow yet. Another was a scenic view of people on the streets in downtown Chicago. The third was a photogenic shot of a high school framed by trees that I took in Wisconsin.

These photos were taken in recent years with a Kodak folding camera that had a very basic lens. Later, in high school, I switched to a CiroFlex twin lens reflex with a full range of f-openings and shutter speeds.

I submitted the entries at the next meeting and quickly forgot about the contest, because I didn't think I had a chance of being a winner. The teacher who ran the photo club said the winners would be announced at the next meeting a few weeks later.

On the day of the next meeting a friend of mine in the club told me that he'd heard I did really well in the contest. I said, "Aw, come on, I don't believe it." I had no such expectations. I sat in the classroom that we used for the meetings that afternoon and the teacher announced the winners. "First prize was won by Herb Wendes." *Wow*, I thought, *that's great*. "Second prize was won by Herb Wendes, also." *What?* I thought. The teacher went on, "And the third prized was won by...guess who? Herb Wendes."

I sat in disbelief and felt a little embarrassed. Was that fair for me to win all three prizes? It just couldn't be. But it was. To this day those have been some of my favorite photographs.

I was busy photographing artistic scenes in black and white around town during the 1940s. I captured artistic scenes of kids hanging around in the neighborhood, of neighborhood streets with old frame houses and hardly any cars parked on them, which are such a contrast with the jam-packed streets today.

I captured artistic scenes of people in downtown Chicago on State Street, Wabash, and on Michigan Avenue; scenes of the exposed railroad trains by Grant Park before they covered them, and of the Lakefront. Pictures were snapped by me and my camera of streetcars, elevated trains, stations, and tracks. I also photographed several schools in Chicago, Lane Tech and Amundsen High Schools, and Waters Elementary School.

The black-and-white photos were taken with a Kodak folding camera using instructions that came with the roll of film and my judgment for the exposure and shutter speed settings. Cameras were not automatic at that time, but I became good at judging the correct settings.

This photo won first place in the photograph contest.

My younger brother Paul with other neighborhood kids

Feeding pigeons in downtown Chicago in 1945

The open train station in downtown Chicago before it was covered

My class at Amundsen High had a few beauty queens, Audrey and Harriet in particular, who were willing models. They were photographed at the Wilson Avenue Rocks along Lake Michigan during the summer months. Hanging around Harry's candy store was the site for pictures of the gang, as well as Wells Park playing baseball on the diamonds, football on the park grass, and muscle-building on outside gymnastic equipment. I snapped pictures of the gang lying around and skylarking on the green grass of the park. I photographed my family and our dachshund like today's paparazzi covers celebrities.

My accomplishments with the camera should have impressed my two brothers, but they didn't pay any attention, nor did they care about my feats. I don't think my parents knew about these successes, either. There wasn't much communication going on with my parents. My stepfather was busy working seven days a week, from early morning to late in the evening, and most of the time my mother was too busy taking care of things at home, as well as in the store.

In addition to my interest in photography, I wrote articles for the Lane Tech weekly newspaper. This was nothing spectacular, just editorial complaints. Lane Tech was overcrowded in the middle 1940s, and had about 6,000 or 7,000 students. They only allowed about four or five minutes between classes, so if your next class was on the other end of the school you practically had to run to get to your locker and then to the classroom. One editorial complaint I wrote was about the mad scramble of students bumping and pushing each other in the crowded hallways. It was like a football gridiron.

Another thing I liked to do as a teenager was ice skate. A noteworthy episode during my first two years of high school at Lane Tech was in the yearly Chicago High School ice skating meet. I think it was in Lincoln Park along Lake Michigan. I entered in a short 50-yard race. I didn't have racing skates with the long blades, I just had hockey-type skates with a stubby front blade. However, they were designed for quick start-ups and stops.

I stood at the starting line with about 10 other contestants who all looked bigger and faster than me, and many who had real racing skates on. The referee said, "Get ready, get set…" and fired a pistol. Off we went. I was skating as if it were a track meet, and I swung my legs out on each side so far that the other guys in the race on either side of me held back so they wouldn't get spiked. I guess I sort of knocked out a couple of the competitors. But it turned out my sprinting paid off and I ended up winning first place in this short race. Again, I greatly exceeded my expectations, and I ended up with a medal and a letter "L" for Lane Tech that was sewn on my myrtle and gold Lane Tech sweater.

Those were the extracurricular activities I was in, but I also held many after-school and summer jobs while in grammar and high school. I will tell you about the "Eighteen Different Jobs During My School Years" in an upcoming chapter, which I did well at— everything from delivering newspapers to working in Chicago's amusement part, Riverview.

In between activities and working at regular jobs when I was going through school, I occasionally had to go to my foster grandparents' apartment building. My grandfather was the janitor, and I helped him shovel snow after bad snow storms. At other times I had to sweep basement laundry rooms or dust banisters in the stairways.

It was a long, boring ride on the elevated train to get to the south side, and took about an hour. As the trains clunkered along the elevated tracks along a stretch on the south side, I amused myself by staring out of the window down at the three-story open back stairways of apartment buildings and at the backyards. Some of the porches were in good shape, but some also had blistering paint and exposed, weathered wood. Junk littered some backyards, as well as old abandoned cars. When the train turned eastward over 63rd Street I viewed all the stores and shoppers. There were also relic old signs about White City, left from the famous 1893 Columbian Exposition.

My grandparents also had a summer home in Round Lake, Illinois, with a gigantic vegetable garden. Every spring and fall my older brother Rudy and I would go there and help dig the garden, rake it, and break up the clumps until it was smooth, fine soil.

Bottom line, between goofing off and getting hurt, I accumulated a lot of experience and knowledge about what was going on in Chicago through after-school activities and the many jobs I took on.

Chapter 5
BRANCHING OUT IN
DIFFERENT SCHOOLS

I attended about five public schools in Chicago. When I was five years old, in 1936, my family lived on the south side of Chicago on Maryland Avenue near Cottage Grove and 63rd Street. I attended kindergarten and first grade at Wadsworth Elementary School, almost a mile walk away. I spoke mostly German at home my first five years and could hardly speak English when I went to kindergarten, so that was a little bit of a learning struggle at first.

We lived on the third floor of a 24-flat apartment building and it was tough to walk up and down the three flights of stairs every time you went anywhere. I don't think there were any elevators in these typical apartment buildings at that time.

A year or so later, we moved from Maryland into a six-flat apartment building about a half mile north, and only a short walk from my mother's foster parents. It was also a three-story structure, but thankfully we rented an apartment on the first floor, and didn't have to trek up and down the stairs anymore. Another benefit of moving was that we were right across the street from the second school I attended, Fiske Elementary, instead of a mile away, as it was on Maryland Avenue.

Oma standing in front of Fiske Elementary School
where I started in second grade

This was also a nicer location since it was closer to the Midway Plaisance Park; a magnificent, narrow, straight stretch of parkland about a mile long between two other large parks. Jackson Park and Lake Michigan bordered on the east end. This was the site of the famed Columbian Exposition, also called White City, in 1893, which transformed Chicago.

On the west end of the Midway was a connection to Washington Park, also a wonderful place in those days. The University of Chicago borders the north side of the Midway.

When we moved to the north side of Chicago, I transferred to my third grammar school, Waters Elementary, near Western and Montrose Avenues. I was about eight or nine years old, just ready to go into the third grade. It was there that I started making my lifelong friendships that lasted on throughout high school, and into adulthood. Many of my relationships were intervened by military service, friends moving to where spouses lived, and their job moves. But most of us are still together and living in the Chicago area.

I started in the third grade at Waters in 1939.

Graduation from 8th grade.
Herb
WATERS SCHOOL JUNE 1945.

Graduation class, Waters, 1945
I'm second from the right in the bottom row.

After graduating from Waters Elementary School in 1945, I started going to the biggest high school in Chicago, Lane Tech. It was a gigantic, three-story, red-brick building on the north side designed by Edward Sullivan, the chief architect for the Chicago Board of Education.

The building and campus covered a whole city block, located on the 3500 block of Western Ave. at Western and Addison. The landscaping and massive grass lawn around the school made it look like a university. I could look out the windows of the inner classrooms at a big courtyard filled with a variety of bushes and small trees when listening to a boring, monotone history teacher.

Lane Tech was strictly an all-boys school for vocational trades and college-bound students. There were about 6,000 students going there when I attended, down from the initial 10,000 or 12,000 students they had when my older brother Rudy attended during the earlier World War II years.

Ventilation was circulated through tunnels in the basement and up through vertical masonry air shafts to all the rooms, with big fans driven by steam engines instead of electric motors. There was no metal ductwork, nor air conditioning.

The cafeteria could only handle about a couple thousand students at a time, so we ate lunch in shifts. There were double cafeteria serving lines on the left and right sides of the lunchroom. Many students brought their own lunches in brown bags and ate at the lunchroom tables. If you didn't bring your own lunch, you waited in long cafeteria lines.

The favorite meal, of course, was hamburgers and French fries, which were served in the cafeteria lines. At the end of the line we put our own mustard and ketchup on hamburgers. This was the time before McDonald's and Burger King; a hamburger was a hamburger—a thick piece of beef on a bun. We also had to pay the full price for everything. Nothing was provided by the city or government.

The administration maintained a strict discipline in the school with student hall guards at every corner of the many hallways. One was careful not to get caught walking around the halls during class time without a pass. Everybody had to be on time and tardiness was not tolerated. After 8:00 a.m., when all classes started, we also had better not be roaming around anywhere outside on the school grounds, or one of the disciplinary teachers, wearing gym shoes, would chase us down and we would be stuck in disciplinary sessions after school.

The schools didn't fool around with wisecracks from any students, either. In the first week of my freshman year there was an episode in our first swim class that mortified all the students.

Let me start by informing you that we didn't wear swimsuits back then, we had to swim naked. Now, on to the story. The frightening episode occurred while being instructed on the rules for the locker room and swimming pool. A mob of students stood in the locker room listening to the instructor. One student made a wisecrack that hit the nerve of a frustrated instructor, who grabbed the student and flung him against the lockers. The student bounced off the lockers and fell on the concrete floor. He was in pain and mortified.

The other students standing there watched in frozen disbelief. I started to tremble in fear. No parents ever came to school complaining about anything.

I can't remember anybody making any smart-aleck remarks after that, or for that matter talking much at all during the swim classes for the whole semester. When we were being lectured in the swimming pool or coming out of the pool, we shivered and were humbled in our nakedness.

Football games in the fall always attracted huge crowds at the Lane Tech stadium against rivals Schuze and Foreman High Schools. It was a little bit of a wild mob in those days. Once, when my brother attended Lane during the Second World War, the students turned a big, red, vintage streetcar weighing many tons over on its side during a big football game rally.

I was almost a straight-A student in my first year at Lane Tech. My German genes were in force for the year, but then my grades and interest in school plummeted during my sophomore year. I guess this happened for several reasons. A severe sinus problem plagued me and I had difficulty concentrating in my classes. I cut school a lot, almost two weeks total during one semester. My parents were fighting and my father planned to separate. All this distracted me, in addition to my negative adolescent attitude and goofing off.

The sinus problem that hampered me was due to an accident playing football a couple of years before high school. In a game, two players on the opposing team pulled an illegal and dangerous defensive maneuver on me. They were blocking me from tackling the ball carrier. One guy behind me hit me in back of the legs at the knees, while the other rammed into me in the front, and I toppled over backwards twisting my body and legs, and crashing onto my head. The horrible end result was that I had a broken nose, which shifted it over a quarter of an inch, and closed my nostrils so that the sinuses couldn't drain properly. Also, a ligament in one knee was torn. I didn't realize at the time what all had happened; I just knew I had difficulty walking home and my nose hurt. I could not blow my nose after that. But, I didn't do anything about the injuries at the time. I felt indestructible, but I quit playing football. No one seemed to notice or care that I couldn't breathe right through my nose or that my sinuses were clogged and couldn't drain. I didn't fully realize what was wrong either, or that my nose had been broken and had shifted over. The trick knee lasted a good 15 years before it got a little better.

It was a few years of clogged sinuses before my mother noticed I was in agony and moping around. An ear, nose, and throat doctor diagnosed the shifted broken nose in my sophomore year, in 1947. He operated on the nose, rebroke it with a hammer and chisel, and shifted it back to where it should be, allowing an opening for breathing and drainage. All this had to be done with only local numbing, without anesthesia. I lay on the operating table and watched and listened to the bone work until I could not tolerate it anymore, and passed out. The doctor then rebroke my nose and moved it back over a quarter of an inch to where it belonged.

The Jig is Up

I accumulated over two weeks of days cutting school in the first two or three months of my sophomore year. Then suddenly I was in the hospital with the nose surgery, and missed school again for a week. The school finally called my father and told him to come to school to discuss the matter of my excessive absences, or I would suffer expulsion and not get credit for the school term.

My father took off work to attend the meeting with the school personnel. They went over the situation...my grades were bad...I wasn't doing all the homework...and I'd missed too many days thus jeopardizing getting credit for the semester. My father said he didn't know about all the absences. They pointed out the absences, and the bad grades were all listed on the report cards, which the parents had to sign. How could he not know about them, since he had signed the reports several times during the semester? My father looked incredulously at the forged signatures. Then it dawned on him that he never saw the report cards nor signed them. The smudges from erasing the number of days absent and bad grades on the report cards and changing them to zero days and higher grades became obvious.

I was relieved that my father was kind enough and didn't say anything about the forgeries to the teachers at the Lane Tech meeting. He just said that I had been sick a lot and maybe I did cut a few days. He promised he would take corrective action with me and they let us go. I got a lecture at home about the importance of school, but my stepfather was disgusted with the situation and let my mother handle me. She was bewildered with my behavior, shook her head, frowned at me, and felt helpless.

I reflected on how my older brother had handled cutting school. One year Rudy worked at a laundry the first three weeks after summer vacation was over and school had started again, because he wanted to continue to earn more money. He had friends tell him what they went over in classes, bring his textbooks home to him, and they handed in assignments that my brother did at home. Some of the teachers thought he was actually in the classroom some of the days.

Chapter 6
THE TREE STARTS TO MATURE

My German genes started to take over a little again when I transferred from Lane Tech to a co-ed high school when I was 16 years old in 1947.

Why did I transfer to another high school, Amundsen, for my third and fourth years? Good question. Not necessarily because it was co-ed. It was because of all the dumb stuff going on at Lane, cutting school, the shenanigans, and my brain clogged with severe sinus problems, which all happened in my freshman and sophomore years. I had to make a big change. At Amundsen, during my junior and senior years, I didn't cut school, I attended all classes, and changed my attitude and did much better in schoolwork again. It was a much more pleasant atmosphere in a co-ed school than the rigid regimentation at the all-boys school, Lane Tech. I felt more comfortable there and a little more confident at Amundsen.

I transferred to Amundsen High School
for my last two years.

51

Transferring high schools helped the transition into adulthood for me. However, the self-awareness had started earlier, before the transfer, during my first two years of high school. I wondered why I really wasn't doing so well. I asked myself, was there something wrong with me? I began to realize some of the antics I was involved with were goofy and childish. I started feeling this was not the best behavior or way to live. I started examining what I was doing, seeing some of my behavior as tricks to get attention, bolstering my weak self-image, or for excitement, without thinking about the consequences.

I felt the anguish of inferior feelings and questionable behavior. I asked my divorced paternal father once when visiting him, what was wrong with me and what I could do about it. He stared at me for a while and struggled for an answer. Finally, he said, "You are too flighty. You jump around from one thing to another impulsively."

I stared back at him with my mouth hung open. "But what should I do about it, Dad?"

"Just don't be so flighty," he said.

"Do you like me, Dad?" I asked.

Again he waited before answering. He was a guy who thought out his answers before speaking. But I caught him off guard. I knew my older brother was his favorite.

"Well, uh, sure I do."

It didn't sound convincing. All I really needed was "you're a good kid and I love you," but the German Americans at that time didn't talk that way or express emotions like that. He didn't recognize my dissatisfaction and helplessness and didn't do anything to relieve it. He had his own problems, such as drinking too much at times, and was not on a positive track with his life.

I thought, *What a coincidence. My stepfather had the same complaint about me.* I was too flighty and didn't stick to things until they were finished. As an example of my own flightiness, I would get a model airplane kit, the kind where you glue a bunch of balsa wood strips and cut-out templates together, and then wrap tissue paper around it. I would go nuts in order to get a World War II airplane, and start building it with a lot of gusto, get the body together, and maybe a wing, then get bored and quit and never go back to it. A month or two later I would get another model plane and never finish it, either. It was more the excitement of getting the new planes and starting to build them than the difficult process of constructing them from start to finish. I was too rambunctious.

It was also during the period when I was 17 years old in 1948, that I started reading the popular "how to" books of the 1940s—which, incidentally, became classics later in the 1900s. I read *How to Win Friends and Influence People*, by Dale Carnegie; *The Power of Positive Thinking*, by Norman Vincent Peale; and *The Art of Plain Talk*, by Rudolph Flesch. These books started to have an influence on my life.

When dealing with people, I learned to smile a little, though it was difficult because I always worried they didn't think much of me. I used their names more, and showed interest in their areas of interest. I learned to develop a little more confidence, to work on some positive thoughts, and eliminate negative ones.

In addition to the above three books, I dug my way through some philosophy books on life that involved Plato, Aristotle, Socrates, and others. In the next chapter we will expose all the experience and knowledge I acquired in the 18 different after-school jobs I had while in grammar and high school.

Chapter 7

BRANCHING INTO 18 DIFFERENT JOBS DURING SCHOOL YEARS

I n 1939, when I was just eight years old, my mother told me I had to start going to work after school. We were still in the Depression years, and weren't loaded with money. I guess that's how things were then. Kids had to help out and work.

However, working after school and summers never let up throughout my grammar and high school years, even after the Depression.

It started with paper routes. My first job was with the *North Center News*, a local paper for the North Center area around the intersections of Lincoln, Damen, and Irving Park Avenues on the north side of Chicago. It only came out on Wednesdays. I would go to where they printed the papers and pick them up for route 21 and deliver them. Then, twice monthly, I had to try to collect money for the deliveries, even though nobody had agreed to pay for the paper to start with. Usually late in the afternoon, when people were mostly at home before dinner, I rang the doorbell and waited for a response on the answer tube, which was on the top of their mailbox. If there was no answer for a while, I would ring again. If there was still no answer, I would move on. Often lights would be on in the apartment or house and you could hear people talking, but they still wouldn't answer the door.

When I caught someone at home and they were willing to answer, they usually asked, "Who is it?"

I answered back feebly on the voice tube, *"North Center News* collecting."

"Who...what did you say?" Most people didn't even know there was a North Center newspaper, much less that there was a voluntary charge. But after a while they became used to my pestering them and trying to make collections.

I would talk a little louder and bolder, *"North Center News* collecting."

Sometimes I got a positive answer.

"How much is it?"

My heart would jump, thinking they might be a paying customer.

"A nickel every two weeks," I'd reply.

The answers varied: "Naw, we are not interested," and "No, don't try again." Some kind hearts said, "Okay, wait a minute." Some people on the second floor would buzz the door open and I would run up the stairs to collect. When they saw I was just a little runt they felt sorry for me and would pay regularly after that. Some would even give me a tip. Other answers I got on the voice tubes were: "You again! You don't give up, do you? Okay. I'll be right with you."

I delivered the *North Center News* for a couple of years until I got tired of it and wanted to make more money. I heard about another local newspaper in another neighborhood that paid more for delivery boys, and you didn't have to make collections. This shopping-type newspaper was entirely free and paid for by the advertisers. It was called the *Lincolnite* and covered the area around Lincoln and Lawrence Avenues, on the north side of Chicago.

The downside was you had to deliver three or four times as many papers, and do it twice a week. It was a long walk pulling my wagon to get to the printing company, where I had to pick up the papers. Then it was another long walk to the neighborhood where I was assigned to make the deliveries. Almost an hour was blown before I ever got started. After I finished the deliveries, it was another 20 minutes to get home. That lasted a month or two. I got tired of the long afternoons and getting home after six o'clock. It was boring, lonesome, and tiring for a little kid, so I quit, and was afraid to tell my mother for a couple of weeks.

My newspaper career went on. I had heard that the *Chicago Tribune* was paying more than twice as much to delivery boys, I think about a half a cent. Since it was a morning newspaper, it had to be delivered early in the morning, around 5:30 or 6:00 a.m. The papers for your route were dumped on a corner near the neighborhood you delivered to. I would pick them up with my red wagon, and cut the bundles open. The problem with this situation was that I had to deliver to specific addresses. It was usually dark at the time and I couldn't always see the addresses on the houses. Plus, being out on the dark street with no one around was spooky. Another problem was I had to go to bed a couple of hours earlier at night, which cut into my leisure time. After three weeks of yawning in classes at school and feeling I was missing out on evening playtime, I gave my notice of quitting.

But that also wasn't the end of my newspaper career. My mother commanded me to find another job. There would be no idle time in the afternoons for me. I then hit what I thought was the big time in newspaper sales. I got a job selling newspapers in a stand on the busy corner of Western Avenue and Irving Park, on the north side not too far from where we lived. You were paid, I think, a penny for every newspaper you sold, which were the afternoon papers in the 1940s, *The Daily News, The Herald Examiner,* and the *Times.*

It was a hectic job. Cars would pull up in front of the stand and the drivers would shout out, *"News!"* or *"Times!"* I would have to run over and hand them the newspaper through the window, and they might give me exact change sometimes, but too often not. Then I would have to fish out the change from my money pouch, which was tied around my belly, and hand it to them. While I was making one sale, frequently another car would toot their horn at me while waiting for the red light to change. I would run over to them. If the light changed in the meantime, they would pull away without a paper, or they would go through the transaction with me while the cars behind them would blast their horns—a nerve-racking thing.

Another problem that occurred with this job was that people

would come by when I was out in the street, take a newspaper, and lay the money down on top of the other newspapers. If they were short a penny or two, or didn't have any small change, it didn't matter; some people took a paper anyway.

In addition to that, when the second or third edition came out in the afternoon, the newspaper delivery truck would try to short-change me. They would claim they gave me 15 papers, but I would count and find only14. They would charge for more papers than they actually delivered. Sometimes at the end of the afternoon I would find I didn't make much money, or even any at all.

I endured it for a month or so, and then decided this was not a job for a young little twerp like myself in a tough newspaper world. So, that was number four of the 18 jobs I had in my youth.

I left the newspaper business and started a new career in grocery stores and delicatessens when I was about 10 in 1941. Down the block from our house, on the corner of Berteau and Western Avenues next to a butcher shop was a National Tea Company grocery store. It was a big chain store in the Chicago area for many years. It was the postwar years and the beginning of the self-service-type stores with carts, which we could push along with us, as it is today. It was also the beginning of the end for many of the Ma and Pa, non-self-service grocery stores, not only in Chicago, but the whole nation.

One day, while I was walking by the National Tea Company grocery store I saw a "help wanted" sign in the window: *Delivery Boy Needed. Afternoons and Saturdays.* I went home and asked my mother, "Do you think that would be a good job for me?"

"Ya," she said with her German accent, "you need a job since you don't sell newspapers on the corner anymore. I didn't like you doing that, anyway."

So, I went to the store and saw the manager. "I would like to apply for the delivery job," I told him.

"Can you work afternoons and Saturdays?" he asked.

"I can be here by 3:30 every day after school and work all day Saturdays," I answered.

"Do you know your way around the neighborhood—not get lost with deliveries, carry heavy bags of groceries upstairs?" he asked.

"Yes, sir. I know all the streets around here—Berteau, Cullom, Campbell, all the streets down to the Chicago River and to Lincoln Avenue on the other side. And I'm strong and am used to carrying heavy things." I knew I wasn't really that strong.

"Well, okay...you can have the job. You will start at 15 cents an hour and you can keep all the tips you make. In between when you are not making deliveries, you can stock shelves, put produce out, sweep floors, carry empty boxes and crates out, and wash windows," the manager told me.

Wow, I thought, *that's a big mouthful of work*, but I quickly said, "I'll take it, sir."

"You're hired. You can start tomorrow at 3:30."

The first couple of weeks I was on time every day, made deliveries, and did a bunch of tasks in between deliveries. Then one day during the third week my parents had something going on, I don't remember what, but I had to miss work that afternoon after school. The manager didn't like it too much, but it was okay.

But the next week on Saturday my foster grandmother insisted that I go out to her country home in Round Lake. It was springtime and the gigantic plot of garden land behind her house had to be dug up and raked to a fine consistency with no lumps in it for planting her annual vegetable garden. I pleaded with my grandmother and mother that I couldn't do it because of the job at National Tea. It didn't mean anything to my grandmother. She shrugged it off.

"Ach, a delivery job is not that important."

This was a family obligation. My older brother and I did it every year and we weren't going to miss this year.

I was afraid to tell the manager on the Friday before that I wouldn't be in on Saturday, and asked my mother to call him on Saturday instead, telling him I was sick and couldn't come in. My mother reluctantly called and said it didn't sound like the manager believed her. My brother and I did the back-breaking digging and raking in Round Lake all day that Saturday and half the day that Sunday and we still weren't done.

The following Monday after school I was at the store promptly at 3:30, despite my aching muscles. I said "hi" meekly to the manager and he gave me a disgruntled look. He said, "Herb, come to the back room with me."

I thought, *Uh-oh!*

He looked down at me. "We are going to let you go. We want someone who can be here all the time. You can pick up your check on Friday."

I looked at him, disappointed and hurt, and words failed me.

I started to become discouraged about working at a young age. So, some time passed by without a formal job, and I forgot about the National Tea experience. I wasn't idle though. I was doing household chores at home such as washing floors, cutting grass, shoveling coal into the boiler, or whatever my parents had me do. When I reached my teens, I found a way of making some really good money in comparison to what I had been making before, and where you got paid right away.

My new job was setting pins manually in a bowling alley. I usually worked on Friday and Saturday nights, because the sessions lasted until 11 or 12 o'clock, which was too late to do on school nights. Plus, that's when the bowling alleys had enough business to hire extra pin setters.

I would walk about a mile from home to the Northcenter Bowling Alley on Lincoln Avenue early in the evening. The sound of bowling balls rolling on the slick varnished alleys, the tumbling pins, and noisy racks crackled throughout the building. Balls thumped on the alleys after being thrown, followed by rolling sounds. I went to the desk and asked, "Do you need any pin setters tonight?"

"Yah. Have you set pins before? Can you handle two alleys?"

"Yes, sir." I hoped he believed me.

"Okay, take alleys six and seven. You get three cents a game."

Picking up the pins and balls in bowling alleys in the 1940s was mostly a manual affair, not automated. I sat upon the back of the alley, legs dangling down, while the bowlers threw their balls. I'd raise my legs when the ball blasted its way through the 10-pin setup so I didn't get hit by any flying pins. After the ball knocked the pins down, I'd jump down into the pit in back of the alley, pick up the ball, and send it rolling down the return rack. The pins were picked up by hand, and laid in the pin rack in a triangular formation. The rack was brought down with an overhead bar and the pins would be standing exactly in the right place in a triangular formation on the alley.

I would get more and more tired as the evening wore on, jumping from one alley to another, bending over picking up pins and the balls, and constantly watching that I didn't get hit with a ball or pins. You got dirty, sweaty, thirsty, and inhaled a lot of dust. The balls and pins pounded out dust from the back pad and side boards of the pit. I would get wearier and forget how many games I set.

Sometimes I was lucky and the bowlers slid some coins down the alley to me as a tip. Finally, it became late and you were not getting any more new bowlers on your alleys. The manager at the desk turned off the lights on alleys six and seven and that meant I could go home. *What a relief. I wonder how much money I made tonight?* The guy at the desk checked the games I set and paid me. *Wow, more than I thought.* When I'd leave the bowling alley, it was dark outside and the streets were mostly deserted. I'd breathe in the fresh, cool air outside. The coins jingled in my pocket. I felt good.

Work or Play?

My mother would never allow my older brother or me not to work after school or during the summers from about eight years old on.

One fall, at the beginning of my sophomore year in high school, I wanted to play football with the Neighborhood Boys Club at a park near where we lived. I worked up the gumption to ask my mother if I could. I had high hopes she might agree. We were alone in the house in the dining room when I asked her. "Ma, I got a chance to play football at the Neighborhood Boy's Club at the park...down the street on Irving Park Road. Is it okay if I play for a couple of months and then go to work after school when it's over?" These were the years my parents owned the delicatessen, when she was working seven days a week from early morning to late evening. During these times my parents also continued their fights, were exhausted, and their nerves were taut.

She looked at me for a while. "I don't dink so. It's not a good idea." Her German accent rang in my ears.

"But why not, Ma? Just this once for a couple of months and then I can look for a job after school. Some of my friends are allowed to play after school and not work."

"No, no, you just go to work...no play every afternoon after school."

"But why not, Ma? Just this once, give me a break." As I begged her more and more, she more stubbornly stood her ground.

"Nein, that's enough now." Her voice was rising.

I started to beg and bawl now. "Pleeeeese, Ma!" I let the tears fall, thinking it might change her mind.

"That's enough. Go to your room." She walked out of the dining room and that was the end of it. And so it went, German genes, German mother. There were times when I could have asked her, if I had been knowledgeable and gutsy enough, "Hey Ma, do you love me or do you just love fighting with Pa and working your head off every day?"

Ironically, I got to play in a couple of football games anyway without her knowing. I said I was going out to find a job after school, but went to the park and signed up for the team instead. In the second game two smart-aleck guys set me up for a clip and I ripped the cartilage in one knee, ending my days of playing football. I hobbled home in pain and was careful not to let them see me struggling to walk. I had a trick knee for at least 15 years. My mother never found out that I played for a couple of games.

And so it went further with my life of work after grammar school. There were a number of different jobs I ended up working at when I was going to high school—some short ones, some longer ones, five total.

One of the short jobs was working as a camera repair assistant for a friend of my parents who was moonlighting at home and was overloaded with work. It was almost an hour ride on the elevated train to his house on the south side. I had to sit listening to the roar, shrieks, and screeching of the trains, and put up with the bumping and jerking. The friend's name was Hans. He was a German with a broad smile, smiling eyes, and slicked-down hair. And a likeable personality. I was flattered and excited to have this opportunity.

My first Saturday morning there he gave me three cameras to repair. "These cameras are not working. I think on this one the shutter is bad. The others, I don't know what's wrong. Look at the tags on them and check them out...see what you can do. Here are some small screwdrivers and wrenches." We were in the basement of his house. "I'll be upstairs working on some other stuff."

I quickly caught him before he disappeared. "Wait, Uncle Hans." He really wasn't my uncle, but that was the custom with the German Americans then. All grown-up men were your uncle. "I'm not sure of what to do...I don't have any experience..."

"Yah, I know...but you are a camera guy...look at the cameras...take some screws out...figure it out. You know what a lens is...a shutter...a diaphragm opening."

It was then I noticed a twitch in his nice smile and how he must be nervous about all the work he had. He didn't have any time to train me. He was relying on my ingenuity and photographic interests, and some miracles. "And don't call me your uncle. You're 13 or 14. I think you're too old for that."

I was dumbfounded and there was nothing else I could do but start to look at the cameras and maybe take them apart. I picked up the camera with the shutter problem. I pressed the lever for cocking the shutter and it seemed to work all right. Then I pushed the button for taking pictures. The shutter opened, it buzzed, and wouldn't close again. *What a predicament.*

I commenced to remove the tiny screws in the face of the camera around the lens. When it was unscrewed the whole lens assembly came out as a unit; the lens, shutter mechanism, and diaphragm (which controls the amount of light that comes in). Now I could turn the whole unit around and see the leaves of the diaphragm and the back side of the lens. The shutter leaf mechanism was still open and buzzing. It looked like the overlapping leaves were stuck. I tried to pry them loose with a screwdriver and kept on pushing the shutter release button. Somehow it suddenly closed.

There seemed to be a pattern as to how the 10 or so leaves of the shutter overlapped in a circular fashion. They had to open and close instantly, whether set at a one second setting shutter speed or 1/500th of a second. I tried to figure out the pattern and removed the super thin delicate leaves that formed the open and closed positions. There were tiny screws that held them in place. It was not a good move. It was impossible to handle the leaves, stick the minute screws back in, and get everything back in place. So, after many hours I decided to let this camera go with all its inner parts lying around, and talk to Hans about it.

I then looked at the other two cameras. One supposedly had light leaking through the bellows that fogged the pictures. On the other one the diaphragm setting lever was stuck. I unscrewed the lens assembly as I did with the first camera and fiddled around with the diaphragm. I felt it wasn't a good idea to take the diaphragm leaves apart again and not get it back together, as with the first camera. So now most of the day was over and Hans came down to the basement and asked how I was doing. I related what I did and showed him the dismantled parts. He was visibly disappointed, but so was I. No help, no instruction manual, no troubleshooting charts.

It was time to go. He paid me a few bucks and said maybe it wasn't such a good idea for me to work under this setup. I left and took the long train ride back on the elevated train. I never went back.

Just before I transferred high schools, from Lane Tech to Amundsen, I had a job at Riverview, an amusement park on Western Avenue, which was ahead of its time. Of the four or so roller coasters there, the Bobs was the fastest, going about 80 or 90 miles an hour down the deepest slope. There were haunted houses, boat rides, parachute drops, a Ferris wheel, a merry-go-round, freak shows, and concessions all over the park. The park bordered the Chicago River on the backside, Lane Tech on the right, and Belmont Avenue on the left.

I worked with another guy at a concession called Spin the Wheel. It consisted of a big, circular table which spun around and had cheap prizes filled in the slots. The participants stood behind a counter that circled the wheel. We spun the wheel and it went round and round. After it stopped spinning, we gave the people playing the game whatever prize the arrow in front of them pointed to.

One slow night my partner and I took turns riding in the Tunnel of Love, which was across from our concession, with girls who came by to play our game. We would strike up a conversation with the girls, and ask them if they wanted to take a ride in the Tunnel of Love. Some were excited to do so. But, much to our surprise, the owner of the concession came by to check on how things were going just when I was taking a ride in the tunnel. When he saw just one guy running the wheel, he asked where I was. My partner said he thought I had gone to the washroom. When I finished my tunnel ride, the owner saw me coming out of the exit, and knew what was going on. He gave us a lecture, and threatened to fire us if we ever did it again.

Since I was working every evening until about midnight at Riverview after a day at school, I was very tired in school, yawning, dozing off, and not being able to concentrate. After a few weeks of this difficult routine and the tunnel episode, I decided this was a good opportunity to quit, and did so.

Yet another job I had was with a photo processing company a few miles north of the Chicago downtown area. Back in the '40s and '50s most department stores, photo shops, and drugstores downtown had a photo processing service but didn't do the work themselves. They had an independent processing company pick up the orders, develop the film, make prints, and deliver the finished order to the store.

My friend Herb, who lived across the street from me, got a job working at Morrey's Photo Processing. His job after school was to lug a big black suitcase on an elevated train to the Chicago Loop and go to his stops, deliver finished orders, and pick up new ones. Typical stops were Bass Photo, Sears, Boston Store, and Marshall Fields. There was an elevated train station right around the corner from Morrey's and stations in the loop near each delivery route.

Morrey was doing very well with his processing service and needed a couple more delivery boys. So, my friend Herb asked our mutual friend Frank and me if we were interested in a job. We both jumped at the opportunity and thought it would be fun working together.

They wanted us there at three o'clock in the afternoon. But since it could take up to a half an hour to get there from school, when we got there we didn't feel like jumping into work right away without refreshing ourselves. We usually all got there a bit after three. After a week or two into the job I became more familiar with things. I decided to stop at the drugstore on the corner across the street. It had a soda fountain, and I ordered a chocolate milkshake or a piece of peach pie because the big black suitcases were heavy to carry around and the routes involved a lot of walking around lugging them for blocks downtown. I needed some energy before starting work. I hoped no one from Morrey's would see me go into the drugstore because it made me a little late for work.

The first time I went into the drugstore I saw someone sitting at the end of the counter and thought, *What the heck, that looks like Frank eating a piece of apple pie.* I walked up to him and asked, "What are you doing here? Aren't you supposed to be at work at three?"

"I always come in for something 'cause I'm hungry after school. What about you, ain't you supposed to be there at three, too?"

We both smiled and laughed at what we were doing. We both continued going to the drugstore most of the days, even though it often meant we would come back a little later from our routes in the Loop, which resulted in some of the daytime workers staying later until we came back. I can't remember if Herb went into the drugstore or not. I don't think he did.

Herb and I enjoyed working with Frank. He was a cheerful, friendly, witty guy who could find something funny about everything. He also had a friendly, appealing smile and quick laughter that brightened up our days. This was ironic because he also had German-born parents, German genes, and a mother that was a stern disciplinarian whom I was afraid of.

Morrey never found out that Frank and I delayed our starting time by going to the drugstore and having a chocolate milkshake or pieces of apple or peach pie. And so, we enjoyed working there.

Walking around in the Chicago Loop when working for Morrey's Photo Processing Company fascinated me. The beautiful lakefront, the crowds on State Street, the big department stores, the hustle and bustle, the bumper-to-bumper traffic and people squeezed into streetcars made it exciting.

For some reason Herb, Frank, and I weren't working at Morrey's anymore in my senior year in high school, so I decided to find another job in the Loop. I heard Carson Pirie Scott needed some stock boys, so I took the el at the Western Avenue station, went downtown, applied for the job and got it—a stock boy in the men's department. The men's department was on the first floor, where they displayed their quality and stylish menswear, and the stockroom was on the sixth floor.

The supervisor of the men's stockroom was a full-time employee named Hank. He was in his 40s, had a wide smile, was a gentle sort of man, and exuded saliva from his mouth when he talked. So, he was always sucking the saliva in between phrases. The assistant full-time stockman was Henry, a red-headed man, with pale white skin and freckles, who was in his 30s. He lived with his mother and things weren't going anywhere in his life. There was another part-time man who was hired when the Christmas rush started, named Joe, who was a slimy kind of guy. He always joked, "I can't wait till I get home tonight. I got a promise from my wife." Then he would give you a *heh, heh* type of laugh, a slimy smile, and his beady eyes watched you closely to see if you laughed or not.

That was the cast of characters in the men's stockroom, but they weren't the ones that provided interesting experiences for me. One day on a break in the employee's cafeteria, sitting along a wall eating a donut, a young woman, slightly plump, about the same height as me, in her lower 20s came up to me. "You are the new guy in the men's stockroom, aren't you?" she asked.

"Yah." I smiled and was flattered with the attention.

She stood in front of me and pressed her two knees on one of my knees. "What's your name?"

She got my attention pretty quick. "Ah...Herb...what's yours?"

"Abegaile. I'm glad to meet you. Hey, why don't you finish your donut and I'll take you up in the women's fur coat stockroom."

I stuffed the donut in my mouth, took a sip more of the coffee and dumped the rest.

She grabbed me by the hand and pulled me right along. "Come on, we don't have that much time...we can have some fun."

We grabbed the freight elevator and went to the 12th floor by the fur coats. A dozen or more rows of fur coats were tightly squeezed together, and you could get lost in them like in a corn maze. There was barely enough room to walk between the rows and no one could see you or what you were doing. Abegaile pulled me into the middle of the coat sections. She pressed her body against mine and said, "Okay, my sweet boy, let's have some fun."

I was a little dumbfounded and nervous. I knew what she meant but I was so shocked, and instead said, "What do you mean?"

"I'll show you." She pulled me closer so I could kiss her.

I was too tense and resisted.

We stood there glued to each other while squeezed between the women's fur coats, silent, nothing happening. She got irritated, "Oh, now look what's happening, someone is coming, probably one of the saleswomen. She'll be looking for a coat for a customer. Let's get out of here," and she yanked me along until we got out of the maze to a corridor. "I've got to get back to work. I might see you tomorrow or some time," she said and she ran off.

I never did see her again. I dreamt of dating her and having some hot affair, but didn't have the guts to contact her.

There was another romantic experience I had at Carson Pirie Scott's a couple of months before Christmas. They were hiring extra elevator operators, one of them being a cute blond girl about 21 years old who had a sparkling, friendly smile. They also added a guy in our menswear stockroom—a dark-haired, handsome, 22-year-old guy, Ralph, to help out during the Christmas season.

The first time I saw the blond elevator operator I became instantly infatuated with her. Every time I had to bring something down to the men's department on the first floor I made sure I took her elevator and I always smiled and said a friendly "hi" to her. She beamed back at me and, being a bit shy, I got nervous. I dreamt of asking her for a date, but I didn't have the courage. I didn't know how old she was, but I figured older than me, and since I still was an adolescent in high school, I wouldn't have a chance.

The new, good-looking guy, Ralph, would have to go down to the men's department on the first floor also as business picked up in the Christmas rush. I asked him if he had seen the nice-looking blond elevator operator. He said he had and that he thought she was really nice.

A month or so went by with Christmas shopping and I thought I'd better do something quick before she might be laid off after Christmas. The next time I caught her with an empty elevator I sputtered out, "Uh, it's been really nice seeing you...I don't know what's going to happen after Christmas...if you will still be here...so I was wondering if we maybe could go out once."

"Oh, that's very nice of you and I do like you...but didn't you hear? Ralph and I are going to be engaged."

"Whaaat? Oh, I didn't know." I was embarrassed, surprised, and couldn't keep the disappointed look off my face. I got off the elevator at whatever the next floor was and said, "Well, okay, see you around."

"Sorry," she said.

I soothed myself by buying a nice dress shirt with a white background and thin green and red vertical stripes, and a pullover sweater with a diamond-shape design in the front that I had been eyeing for some time at the 20 percent employee discount. These were the nicest items of clothing I felt I ever owned up to that time, and I put the two women out of my mind.

I bummed around at a few jobs after graduating from high school. The first one was at a powder puff factory for a few weeks early in the summer of 1949. I got the job accidentally and immediately regretted it. A friend told me about a company that was hiring on Irving Park Road. I couldn't find it right off and went into the wrong building. I told the owner I was looking for work and he said he needed somebody and hired me.

It was a dusty, stinky, sweaty place during the humid hot days in Chicago. I was peeling plastic, powder-puffy sheets off of piles which stuck together, hundreds in each pile. Also part of my job was to feed the plastic cutouts to women who were at machines, stitched them together into powder puff holders, and put stamped snap buttons on them. I also had to sweep the floor and clean things up in the dumpy atmosphere. The boss was thrilled to get some kid with German work genes and work ethics to do the work; a kid afraid to be seen not working.

It was a hot July day; there was no air conditioning in the sweat shop and only a few fans were blowing air around. It was drudgery to get up early in the morning and be at work at eight o' clock. I was used to freer summer vacations while in grammar and high schools, even though I usually had some kind of job.

I wanted to dump the job, but I was afraid to tell the owner, especially since he had given me a raise after the first couple of weeks.

I considered just not coming in, but I was afraid I might get gypped out of some pay. After three weeks, one bright sunny morning, I built up the courage to go in, because I couldn't stand the idea of another day of sweating and breathing in the dusty atmosphere. I went into his office the first thing in the morning and spoke so quietly that he almost didn't hear me. "Ah…this isn't the kind of job I wanted after leaving high school. I'm going to quit."

It took a moment before it registered on him. "Why?" He spoke in a soft tone. "There were no complaints about you…all the women on the machines like you, and I even gave you a raise. I would like you to stay."

"No," I murmured, "this isn't what I want. I'm going."

Then he looked angrily at me. Even though he wanted me to stay, he wasn't about to negotiate with an ungrateful teenager off the street. I stammered, "Can I get paid for my hours…"

He said I'd get my check on Friday, the regular time everyone got paid. Wow, I was relieved he wasn't going to make a fuss over that.

Now I didn't have a job and there was still the rest of the summer of 1949, not to mention my whole life and starting some kind of career. I was 18 and had no prospects of a trade or education.

My school buddy Norb, who I palled around with and shared a locker with in high school, was already working as a bricklayer, which he started right after he graduated from high school. He told me they needed a laborer to build scaffolds, pile bricks and blocks on them, and mix mortar and keep the brick layers supplied.

"It pays big bucks, and you will be working with me and Frank, mostly on houses in the north suburbs of Chicago."

The idea of making five or 10 times as much as I was making in the powder puff factory excited me. I said, "You're darn right I want the job," although I didn't know anything about laboring and had no idea what an exhausting job it would be.

It was still July. The sun was bright, it was hot, and the humidity was high on my first day as a laborer. I was working for a brick mason contractor and had to serve four bricklayers trying to lay bricks and blocks as fast as they could. My friend Norb showed me how to mix mortar. First I had to shovel the mortar mix, which was a sludge of sand and water, from a large container into the mortar mixing pan along with a certain amount of dry cement powder. Then I took the mixing hoe and thoroughly mixed the cement into the mortar mix by pulling the hoe forward and back. Not an easy task, but I started off with a lot of enthusiasm.

Norb then showed me how to build the scaffolding for when the walls got higher. Connect the end and cross tubes together, and put thick, heavy, wood planks on top. Wow. I really needed muscle power to do this.

"After the scaffolding is built and the planks are laid, load piles of brick and blocks at each bricklayer's station," Norb instructed.

I could barely lift the thick blocks, much less raise them up to scaffold height. The rough concrete of the blocks was abrasive and started to wear through my gloves and played havoc on my hands. Having done what I had been instructed to do, I then had to shovel the previously mixed mortar up onto each bricklayer's mortar board.

Norb told me, "Never let the bricklayers stand around without their supplies. The boss is one of the bricklayers, and he knows what's happening."

All day long I was behind the demands of the four bricklayers, who were starting to scream at me. "More mortar, bricks, block...move my position down...the mortar is too thick...too thin...get going, Herb!"

"The next batch of mortar isn't ready yet," I protested. "I'm the new guy, give me a break."

They were used to experienced laborers who knew how to coordinate everything. Experienced laborers could pace themselves so they wouldn't slow down or drop from muscle fatigue and exhaustion. The four bricklayers put up with me the first week or two, but after that they were totally intolerant. I think they liked to badger me.

Every night I got home, showered, ate dinner, and went to bed at seven o'clock because I couldn't keep my eyes open. I hoped that I would get faster, more proficient, and that my muscles would get stronger. But just the opposite happened. I was getting more tired, and weaker as I went along. I couldn't recuperate fast enough one day after another. However, when I got my first paycheck, I got this unbelievable pay which I had never earned before.

I got a little better, but nowhere as good as an experienced laborer, and I still got angry stares and remarks from the boss. My weekends were lost, too. I was in no shape to do anything. Along about the third week I began to think about dumping the job, which I wasn't cut out to do as it was. Like with the powder puff job, I thought three weeks was enough of this torture. I asked my mother if it was okay to quit.

"You are really making a lot of money...are you sure you can't get through for at least the summer?"

I didn't argue or plead with her to let me quit. I knew what I had to do. On Friday afternoon I told Norb to tell the boss that I was quitting. Nobody had any arguments about it and I went back to a normal life.

During that first summer out of high school my parents suggested they were not anxious to send me to college, and felt it probably would be a waste of money. Furthermore, I should work with my hands in a job such as a carpenter. At Lane Tech High School I had taken a number of industrial courses, such as wood shop, foundry, and print shop. So I decided I might give the printing trade a shot as a career job.

My foster grandparents knew somebody who helped me get a job at a letter press company in Printers Row, just south of Chicago's downtown area. It was another dirty, dusty, smelly place. They started me off with dismantling old jobs, which were manual setups of individual pieces of type. These old jobs had been lying around for the past few years because none of the experienced typesetters wanted to do the job, even though the type in them needed to be reused. I sorted the individual letters by type and size and put them in their designated drawers. Strips of spacers, called slugs, were sorted according to thicknesses and length and put where they belonged. A boring and grimy job, but not the apprenticeship training at setting up jobs initially, which I wanted. They just wanted me to clean up the junk, which the typesetters didn't want to do. But after a while I got the old setups dismantled and cleaned up the old junk pile.

Then, slowly, I became an all-around guy in other departments. When they needed help in running the hand-fed presses, like the Gordons, they showed me how and I did it well. Then they needed help in bindery folding, stitching, collating, and so on, and I did well again. Nate, who was a relative of the owner, needed help packaging orders in the shipping department. I went in and did a neat and quick job of packaging stacks of printing for shipping. Nate, a short, nervous guy, was overjoyed when they put me in the shipping department to help him out.

But printing wasn't destined to be my career choice either, nor did I envision myself as a skilled craftsman in a factory, and I had no intention that I would let it be. At the time my parents owned a small delicatessen near Lincoln and Addison Avenues. They sold the big delicatessen on Western and Berteau the year before. My mother ran the store during the day. My father had bought a Dr. Pepper franchise and was delivering soda pop. After four or five months of integrating myself at the printing company, my mother got sick and had to go to the hospital. I was needed to run the store for a couple of months. My father was working at his Dr. Pepper soft drink deliveries and my older brother was going to college during the day. We couldn't close the store, so that left me to run it and I was selected to save the day. I explained the situation to the printing company and that I wanted to take a leave of absence. They said they really wanted me back in a couple weeks, not months, but reluctantly gave me a leave of absence.

While working at the store for those two months, as my mother recuperated from her surgery, I decided I wasn't going back to the printing company. I didn't like the idea of having black ink embedded in the skin of my hands and under my fingernails for the rest of my life.

Adulthood Starts to Sink in Further

While still working at the store, I started taking night classes at Wright Junior College (a Chicago city college) and was doing very well. When my father came home from his pop route he would wash up and eat, then take over the store during the evening hours, relieving me from the day shift.

Going to junior college was a positive and worthwhile step in my life. I found out I excelled at college courses and academics, and that I had the German gene for organization. I took English Composition, Economics, and German and was near the top in all my classes. It was the beginning of my education as a professional, though I didn't know what it would be at that time, nor did I believe it would happen—but it felt good. My life started to take a complete U-turn. My German work genes took over, and I plowed ahead in my academics like a powerful steam locomotive.

Chapter 8

TOUGH FAMILY YEARS

We moved from the south side of Chicago to the north side. My stepfather bought a three-bedroom house—a bungalow on the north side of Chicago in 1938, for $4,000. It was built in 1904, and had a full basement and two large attic bedrooms. My older brother Rudy and I slept in the front attic bedrooms in a queen-size bed. The main floor consisted of an enclosed porch in the back, a kitchen, the only bathroom, a dining room, a master bedroom where my parents slept, a living room, another bedroom in the front of the house where my younger brother Paul slept, and a front entrance and a porch. It stood on a narrow, 30-foot lot.

The house had a coal furnace in the basement and gravity ducts feeding up into the rooms. You had to manually shovel coal into the boiler to heat the house and for hot water. The boiler would have to be stoked at night, the burnt coal clinkers broken apart, and the ones that were burnt out had to be removed. Then enough new coal would have to be shoveled into the boiler to last during the night and the draft level set to low for a lower level of heating. The walls in the house would get coated with coal soot in the air and have to be cleaned every three or so months during the heating season.

To get a new load of coal into the coal bin in the basement was a major, back-breaking operation. The coal delivery truck would dump the load of coal in the alley into a big pile. Then this mountain of coal had to be shoveled into a wheelbarrow, and one load at a time, wheeled through the backyard, downstairs into the basement, and then wheeled to and dumped into the coal bin in the middle of the basement. It was a miserable job and we inhaled gobs of coal dust doing it.

WWII Starts, Pa Gets Defense Job

Up until the early WWII years my stepfather was a bartender at the Bismark Hotel in downtown Chicago. He quit his job to work in a defense plant, Foot Gear Works, as an inspector with much better wages and lots of overtime hours. He didn't have a background of machine shop work, but they trained him how to use measuring instruments such as micrometers and calipers. He did well because he was particular and thorough. If the part was five thousandths of an inch off, or whatever the tolerance for accuracy had to be, he caught it and would not let the part get through inspections.

Ma and Pa's Fights

My older brother Rudy and I slept in the attic bedroom of the bungalow that faced the street on Berteau Avenue for about 10 years from 1939 until 1949, from when I was about eight years old until I was 18. Some nights my older brother Rudy and I would go to bed in our upstairs bedroom, and we were awakened by an eruption of loud arguing by our mother and stepfather downstairs. Our parents slept in the master bedroom below us on the first floor and they were usually still up when we went to bed. The argument would escalate quickly. My stepfather had a quick temper in his younger days. It made us shudder in bed. After some more shouting back and forth he would stomp through the house to the back door and slam it on his way out.

After he left, everything would be still. Rudy and I were shocked, confused, and afraid. We were afraid to go downstairs to see how my mother was doing. I'm sure she needed some comfort and support. Unfortunately, we didn't have enough rapport with her; we couldn't communicate our feelings well—just didn't know what to say. The word "love" embarrassed us. Our parents otherwise were good people, but they lived with anger, frustration, fighting and worked like maniacs in their marriage at that time.

We lay in our bed and hoped our stepfather would come back soon. But after a while, after not hearing anything, we fell asleep and never heard him when he came back. We believed he walked around the block a few times to simmer down, or went to the neighborhood tavern on the corner where the owner was a German and a friend of his, and who he liked talking to. Presumably, after he calmed down, he came back sometime later in the night, because the next morning when I walked into the kitchen he was there. I was embarrassed and didn't know whether I should say hello or be quiet. I couldn't look him straight in the eye, but I meekly said good morning. He answered in what sounded like a friendly tone, but his expression belied his feelings and his frustration with the situation. He was quiet, didn't say any more, and shortly left for work.

Rudy and I prayed that the fighting between them would stop, but it didn't until our stepfather decided to separate from my mother and move out, leaving my mother and us three boys alone in the bungalow. He rented a small, furnished apartment in another part of Chicago and continued as a defense worker at the gear company. We went through a few tense, sad months of estrangement. He made sure we had enough money to live on, and called and checked on how we were, but my mother was distraught. She wanted Paul to come back home. She needed help with the three boys. We were no picnic. So, she talked to us, Rudy, Paul, Jr. and myself, and told us she wanted us to visit my stepfather and ask him to come back.

My mother arranged for us to go there, so we went to his apartment one night and said, "Won't you please come back home, Pa?"

Tears flowed in his eyes and he was in torment. He couldn't and wouldn't say no. He decided to try and make a go of it again. He knew he had a bad temper and would try to control it more. He knew my mother was a good woman, though difficult at times and stubborn, and that we kids were really okay, just a little mixed up.

I didn't really understand what was wrong at the time, but it became clear to me recently. They were a mismatched couple. They had a personality conflict, had lived different lifestyles growing up, were of different religions, and came from different backgrounds. My mother was brought up in poverty as an orphan. She was a Lutheran. She had been married before, was divorced, and had two children. My stepfather came from a devout Catholic family in Bavaria, Germany. They didn't believe in divorce. They were middle class Germans and professionals. The marriage just didn't click well for them during those years.

Family Goes Into Delicatessen Business

Things went somewhat better for three years during the war with my stepfather back home. He made more money than he ever did with about 10 hours of overtime pay a week at the defense plant. And he had some time off for the family and taking care of the house.

However, in 1944, when I was 13 years old, he decided to go into business for himself. It was his dream to own a business, and be a salesperson as he had been trained in Germany. He bought a delicatessen on the north side of Chicago, just down the street from our bungalow. It was a fairly large store for a Ma and Pa affair— fresh vegetables and fruit in the front by the window, a cigarette and candy counter off on one side, a newsstand by the corner door, bread and noodles in an island in the middle, and refrigerated German deli cabinets in the back of the store.

Most of the groceries we had to get off the shelves for the customers (because it wasn't self-serve), such as canned goods, cereals, and milk. There were no carts. The items they wanted were piled up on a long counter where the prices were added up with a crank-driven adding machine.

Pa's first delicatessen on Berteau and Western, late 1940s

My mother made German and American potato salad and prepared baked and boiled hams. They also sold some German and American cold cuts and sausages, along with a full line of groceries, but they weren't an exclusive German-type delicatessen. It was a mixed bag of German and American stuff. My older brother and I worked in the store after school at times, delivering groceries, stuffing newspapers, restocking shelves, and sometimes waiting on customers when things were busy.

In 1948 my father did some good wheeling and dealing. First, he saw that he could sell our bungalow, which we had owned for about 10 years, for triple the amount he paid—$12,000 versus the original price of $4,000. He put the house on the market and got his price.

However, the Ma and Pa store grocery businesses started to suffer as self-service chain grocery stores with carts began to expand. Because of this, he saw it was a good time to sell the store on Berteau and move into another venture. He bought two Dr. Pepper delivery trucks and a franchise covering the near north side of Chicago. At the same time he bought a small grocery store near Addison and Lincoln

Avenues on the north side for my mother to take care of. We moved into a nice, big apartment above the store.

My parents worked seven days a week, as Ma and Pa stores did then, from early morning to late in the evening. My father worked all day delivering the heavy cases of pop around and then came home and took care of the new small grocery store in the evenings. They hardly ever had any time off and were continually stressed out, mixed up, and dead tired. And their fighting increased and decreased accordingly with the work stress.

Pa's New Car Wrecked

Of course, there were other stress factors such as myself and my brothers. My father finally was able to buy a new car as the auto companies started manufacturing them again after the war, around 1950. He traded his big, sleek, stylish 1939 Buick for a brand new, apple green Dodge. He was proud of the car and revered its newness.

Then of course, we kids wanted to drive the car. I never got a chance because I bought an old green 1938 Ford when I graduated from high school. It had about 250,000 miles on it and it was driven into the ground during the war years because they stopped making cars for a long time. It was a disaster and burnt oil like a furnace.

But, Rudy got to drive the new car at times. He told me that it's only by the grace of God that he's still alive with his occasional drinking and driving at the time. When he was 21 years old, driving home from a bowling alley about midnight, after drinking a couple beers during the league games, he had a major accident. He was dead tired from the week, from his classes and studies at the engineering college he went to, and from his part-time job. He drove into a triple main street intersection and fell asleep right in the middle of it. The car moved on into the following side street, careened off of cars parked on both sides of the street, and smashed head-on into a tree.

My stepfather answered the call from Ravenswood Hospital shortly thereafter, letting us know Rudy had had a bad accident, smashed up the car, and was hospitalized. We were paralyzed. My father went to the hospital immediately to see Rudy and find out how badly he was injured, and whether he would live at all. Miraculously, he didn't have any broken bones, but he had many cuts and bruises and was bandaged up. He could talk. My father told him not to worry about the car, which a tow truck took somewhere. The police report said it looked as though the car was totaled.

My father's prize beauty was badly damaged. However, they were able to put new fenders, a hood, and doors on the car and to somewhat straighten out the frame. It looked nice when the repairs were done, but the warped frame was a problem and the car pulled a little to one side. So much for my father's proud ownership of a new car and reducing stress on my parents' relationship and workload.

My parents learned about how to get along better and mellowed as they got older. Finances were good and they were able to buy bigger and better houses over the years. They slowly became proud of their three sons and their accomplishments, despite their own difficult relationship.

Part II

GROWING UP IN THE SHADE OF
THE GERMAN CULTURE

Chapter 9
GRANDMA BRAINWASHED ME
LIFE IN THE U.S. FOR MY FOSTER GRANDPARENTS

I t was a different world in Chicago in the 1930s and '40s. There was very little traffic on the streets; not many cars around at all. Sometimes there was only one car parked on the whole block that I lived on. Kids would play baseball or touch football on the side streets. When a car came down the street, the kids slowly stepped to the side and the car in turn drove by slowly. They waited impatiently and jeered at the driver. Sometimes the driver yelled back, "Why don't you play in the park?"…but in a friendly way.

View looking down Berteau Avenue

Not many cars around back then.

Streetcars clanged their bells and their wheels click-clacked on the rails. Electric elevated trains rumbled and roared up above the streets and went down to street level farther out. The different lines rose out of underground tunnels, which ran in all directions north, south, east, and west. Public transportation took you to work, school, downtown, shopping, to the beach, dance halls, Riverview Park; wherever you wanted to go. Movie theaters were all over, mostly within walking distance from where you lived. If a family went to see a double feature at the movies in the evening, and had to walk home when it was dark around 11 o' clock or midnight, they weren't afraid; the neighborhoods were safe.

There were German restaurants, butcher shops, and grocery stores, as well as delicatessens all over the place. There were some German movie theaters. German singing clubs, social clubs, and soccer clubs were scattered all about. People could take German speaking classes in public or private schools. Some churches preached in German as well as English. Neighborhood people sat on their front porches when it was warm and said hello when you walked by.

Those were the pleasant things about Chicago in those days. But of course, I still had my problems. My grandmother brainwashed me during my childhood. When I visited her as a child and we were alone, she would often tell me how things were so much better in Germany than in the United States. She stared straight at me, pursed her lips, and said, "The apples in Germany are bigger and better. The apples are nicht so gut here in America."

I looked at her in awe. I wished I could experience one of those tender morsels. And then, in later years when I was sent to Germany for military duty, I had a chance to eat a German apple. I found out that some of the apples were smaller, greener and a little bitter in Germany.

Oma, as many Germans called their grandmothers, was what we called her. She was not really my grandmother; rather, she was my mother's sponsor when my mother immigrated to the U.S. She had no direct relationship to my family. She wasn't able to have children, so she was like a mother to my mother, and became like a foster grandmother to my brothers and me over the years.

Oma and Opa's first Christmas in Chicago as immigrants

I had the same relationship with her as with my parents. My older brother Rudy was her darling and she only put up with me. She developed prejudices in me against the American style of living and frequently compared the German lifestyle to the American lifestyle. I represented Uncle Sam's little nephew and she dumped her frustrations on me. Her complaints to me about Americans were, "The people here are sort of lazy…not so clean…and they don't have good manners like the German's have." I was somewhat influenced by these comments. I thought all my German American relatives and their families were the best people in the world and the American neighbors were inferior and sort of slobs. I had to grow up first before I could admit to myself that granny was prejudiced. My feelings were mixed up and confused at the time.

She was an energetic woman with many abilities. She was organized, frugal, punctual, decisive, and faced problems head-on and got things done. She was diligent, industrious and hard-working. In German they have one word that describes these traits: *Fleizick*.

I remember when we would eat with them in their sunken janitor's apartment on the south side of Chicago in the 1930s and '40s. We ate in a big, old-fashioned kitchen. The refrigerator had the round condenser on top, the kitchen sink stood on legs and was open underneath, and the old, boxy oven was also open underneath, standing on legs. The pantry was long and half the size of the kitchen. You could store home-canned foods in it; a whole winter's worth. There was a small window high up in the kitchen wall that almost went up to the ceiling, which looked out at the sidewalk and street. When you sat at the table eating you saw the legs of people walking by. I got the feeling that I was a small, underground person, not part of the big people world.

Oma could make a kitchen cutting knife razor sharp with a sharpening rod. I was mesmerized by watching her quick, rhythmic, back and forth movements between a knife and the rod, and in no time the knife was dangerously sharp. She then took a big round loaf of rye bread in her one hand, held it against her body and sliced even pieces as if she were an automatic bread slicing machine. To this day, try as we may, neither my wife nor myself have mastered Oma's knife sharpening skills and cutting even slices of rye bread.

Oma in the latest style in 1928

She could also whip up Depression-type dinners; pancakes with applesauce or jelly, farina with cinnamon sprinkled on it, potato soups that didn't taste bad, one-pot string bean meals with potatoes, and spinach with scrambled eggs.

She was a fluent conversationalist in German, a storyteller, and a little opinionated and outspoken. She was somewhat taller than the typical woman, had an average build, but with firm muscles. High cheekbones, a pointed nose, an infectious smile, and an endearing laugh made her a likeable personality. She was kind, intelligent, and entertaining. On the other hand, she was also a perfectionist, somewhat domineering, and a proud, prejudiced German.

How could I, a little runt of a kid, doubt her wisdom and power?

I guess she had her problems too, and was trying to find her place in this country, which seemed so different and strange to her.

But Opa, one of 10 children, was of a different nature, not one who would brainwash anybody, as was the case with Oma. As with Grandma being called Oma in Germany, my grandpa was also called Opa. When they arrived in the U.S. from Germany in 1927, Opa had a regular trade which he had learned in Germany. However, in Germany he also was an entertainer, a magician, illusionist and hypnotist on the stage, on the side.

One of his brothers, Fritz, who immigrated here a few years earlier, sponsored him. Fritz was a janitor in an apartment building on the south side of Chicago. He didn't get Opa a job that was in his trade or as a magician on the stage, but rather got him what was available at the time—a job as a janitor, also in a three-story apartment building at 62nd Street and Ingleside, near where he lived.

Opa was a quiet, gentle, and humble man with a lot of talent. He had somewhat of a slim build and not a lot of muscle strength. Unfortunately, the janitor's job was grueling. He had to shovel coal into the boiler for heat and hot water, shovel mountains of coal delivered and dumped out on the street into wheelbarrows, and wheel them into the basement boiler room. He had to carry the garbage down from the back porches in a barrel, which he lugged on his back from the third floor down. He had to repair electrical, plumbing, and steam piping problems. He had to cut the grass in spring, summer and fall, and shovel snow in the winter.

He did his janitor's job diligently, but his passion was pioneering photography in the 1930s. He bought a stereo camera and a big French stereo viewer; he bought a 16 millimeter movie camera and projector; plus, he equipped himself with developing and printing equipment and an enlarger. He developed his own black and white films, and made prints. He filmed the 1934 World's Fair in Chicago and put together a 16 mm movie of it, including Sally Rand's risqué nude fan dance, where she swished fans back and forth to hide her body.

Five years passed by living in the "apartment neighborhood" on the south side while he did his back-breaking janitorial work and worked on his photographic interests in whatever leisure time he had. He did his job without complaining and he reluctantly became somewhat used to life in America.

However, Oma was not satisfied with living in a janitor's apartment in Chicago. She decided they needed to build a summer home that they could go to on weekends and chose one 60 miles north of Chicago in Round Lake. Their plan was to eventually move out there full-time to get away from inner city crime and the beginning of decay, and to live out in the country.

They bought lumber and a plot of land in Round Lake, Illinois for only 650 dollars in 1932. German friends, who were craftsmen, came out on weekends and helped him build the summer home. They dug out the trench for the cement block foundation by hand and laid the block with mortar. They hammered the 2 x 8 joists together for the floors, ceilings and roof, the 2 x 4 studs for the walls, and boards for the floors and roof. They drank beer while they worked and at the end of each rugged workday ate a big roast, which the Frauen made over an open fire. Someone who had the knowledge did the electrical work, while those with the heating and plumbing work skills did their specialties. Plaster boards were nailed on the walls, finished off and painted.

Oma and Opa's summer home in Round Lake, Illinois

Afternoon coffee and cake, a German tradition

It was a big plot of land and the back half was a large vegetable garden. Oma would grow vegetables and fruit, pickles, beans, spinach, beets, tomatoes, strawberries, and a lot more. She canned enough to last until the next year's harvest. This was all done before they would board up the summer home for the winter. She loved the area. She planted flowers all over the place, nice trees, hedges around the front, put in a fence, and evergreen trees were carefully placed. They added on and remodeled what was originally a 650-dollar summer house into a beautiful chalet-like house.

My brother Rudy and I had to dig up the gigantic vegetable garden every spring and fall. Later, when Paul was old enough, he had to help also. It would have to be done at exactly the right time in spring. The lumps had to be broken down and the dirt raked into a fine mix. We tried to hide the big lumps of dirt by raking the fine stuff on top, thus hiding them. But Oma's quality control instincts didn't let that type of shirking of duty get by her. We couldn't go home until it met her stringent criteria, which meant we would be spading and raking the entire weekend and left with sore arms, necks, and leg muscles.

I'm spading Oma's gigantic vegetable garden
in Round Lake under her supervision.

She invited all her friends and relatives for coffee and cake in the German tradition on weekends. They sat outside in the charming surroundings sipping and smelling the aroma of freshly ground coffee. It usually was too hot to drink at first so they poured some in the saucer and sipped it slowly from the plate. They ate German-style pound cake with powdered sugar sprinkled on top, or strawberry shortcake with genuine, freshly made whipped cream. She made a close friendship with a neighbor, as well as entertaining her German American friends.

The little house turned out to be Oma's hideaway from the city for years. They left the city on weekends and on vacations, and enjoyed their summer home in Round Lake in the '30s and '40s. All the while, their nice apartment neighborhood on the south side of Chicago was changing, going downhill from its original exclusiveness of the 1920s. There was more and more crime and the neighborhoods became unsafe.

One Christmas Oma was shopping on 63rd street near Cottage Grove. As she was walking out of a clothing store she heard someone shouting, "Stop him, stop him!" The robber ran past her, turned, and fired a gun at the guy chasing him. She was right in the line of fire and instead of the bullet hitting the store manager, the bullet went crosswise through the back of her coat—in and out—fortunately, without injuring her.

Three years in a row burglars also broke into their apartment while they were on vacation in Round Lake. The burglars would watch when people were gone for a length of time, and then break into the apartments. Oma called us up when they returned from a vacation to come and look at the mess. I saw how the burglars dumped the contents of all the dresser drawers on the floor, and threw everything from the closets and storage rooms all over the place. When they returned from vacations they would go nuts with frustration, feeling deeply insulted over the mess in their home and the intrusion into their privacy.

They weren't able to move to Round Lake full-time until 1955, five years before my Opa's retirement, because of the difficulty in finding a job there. They drove 60 miles one way, over an hour and a half, to get from their apartment in Chicago to Round Lake nearly every weekend except in the winter.

Opa finally connected with a job as a janitor at a grammar school in Round Lake. They left the strife of a declining neighborhood on the south side of Chicago and moved out to their chalet in Round Lake. Some years later he retired, but only enjoyed his retirement for a few years thereafter. He was hit with the scourge that people dreaded. He smoked heavily most of his life, as was the custom of the times, and he developed cancer in the brain. He received treatment, was in the hospital, and was sent home with no hope.

I remember when we visited them, I stared at him sitting in an easy chair in the corner of the living room, holding his head in excruciating pain, his face wrenched up, moaning—probably wishing he were dead and wondering what he had done to deserve this. It wasn't long before he passed away in 1960 at the age of 67. He was born in Bremerhaven in 1893.

Oma was in turmoil over Opa's death. Her lifestyle was her passion, her husband was her reason for living. He was a quiet, unassuming gentleman with great skills who ended up struggling most of his life with janitorial work. Grandma was in a trauma. She wrote a letter before she passed away to my mother, blaming her for hanging on to her too much, for not letting her live her own life. My mother felt Oma was ignoring her. Oma had a strong, close relationship with other friends and one certain neighbor. Despite my mother's concern and hard work helping Grandma out during her bereavement, it actually put a sort of wedge between them. In remorse, my foster grandmother died before the year was over. She was 68, a year older than Opa, born in Dessau, Germany in 1872.

My mother was decimated with guilt and grief after Grandma died and she read the letter. She suffered from depression because she felt it was her fault. It took a couple of years before she got over it and went back to a normal life.

Chapter 10

SANDWICHED IN BETWEEN MY TWO BROTHERS

I was the middle guy in my German family, sandwiched in between my older brother, Rudy, and a younger brother, Paul. They were the hot shots, or so I viewed them at the time when I had a distorted self-image, and I guess you might say I was seen as the blooper shot in. My older brother, born a few years before me in 1928, was a neat, well-behaved, intelligent, lovable toddler. As a toddler, when I was born, he arranged all his toys neatly, and played quietly by himself. My parents and grandparents were the proudest people in the world the first couple years after he was born. The prodigy child was *wunderbar*.

I came along a few years later in 1931 and blasted things apart. The only way I could get any attention was to raise some ruckus, like busting up Rudy's toys, forts, and soldiers. My elders weren't too happy about that, but I needed some attention and affection, too. Unfortunately, people didn't know much about psychology in those days and they concluded I was a mischievous little devil.

Then some six or seven years after I was born, in 1937, my mother and stepfather had a child together. My younger brother, Paul, entered the scene. By this time some of the Old World German beliefs, strictness, and frugality in our family had eased up. Paul only ate certain foods that he liked and ate them almost exclusively; hot dogs, peas, and baloney sandwiches were some things on his restricted menu. My parents suddenly and miraculously didn't force Paul to eat everything on his plate the way they made Rudy and me do when we were kids, and you might say, he got away with it. In adulthood he improved his eating habits—he developed a strong preference for pizza and eats it frequently.

Also, when I went to high school I had two pairs of good pants hanging in the closet. By the time Paul entered high school he had maybe 15 pairs of good pants. Also, much to my dismay, he also didn't have to work after school as I did from eight years old onward. As far as I know, Paul was a diligent student and didn't cut school. In my narrow view and limited knowledge about people, I felt I was stuck between two prima donnas, but as the German philosophers say, "Das Leben ist nicht Gerecht" (life is not fair).

Paul, of course, was the other side of the sandwich I was squeezed in between. Another way to say it was that I was the liver sausage in between two slices of pumpernickel bread, so to speak. So anyway, the point here is that in order for me to get anywhere in this hot shot squeeze I had to try a lot harder and sort of do it on my own. Probably my parents share some of the blame because they didn't give me much psychological support or understanding. They had me convinced that I should be a janitor, or at best a carpenter's assistant. You know, work with your hands, not your brains. Let your brothers do the mental jobs. I had to overcome this image of myself being second rate to my siblings. When I went to school in the '30s and '40s there wasn't much in the way of IQ or achievement tests given out, so you didn't know whether you were a whiz kid or a dummy.

Thus, my self-worth was rather low during the growing-up years as I floundered around and indulged in some misdirected activities. However, as stated before, it was not all negative. I got through grammar and high schools zigzagging up and down from top grades to bottom grades. The reader will recall I participated in some extracurricular activities in school and did well at them. I managed to perform well in the 18 after-school jobs I had during my school years, and I survived the problems my parents had with each other in our home.

Herb and his brothers, Rudy and Paul, in 1937

Herb, Rudy, and Paul in recent years

Rudy had a slightly slim face, a trim build, and a confident smile when he was growing up, which let people know he knew what he was talking about. He made you feel like he was sharp. He was popular and wasn't afraid of girls, even though he wasn't a Casanova. He was a serious student, paid attention in class, did all his homework, and got top grades.

I don't want any misunderstanding here about my two brothers. I have the utmost respect and admiration for them. They are both first-rate brothers. We are the best of friends in our adulthood and enjoy each other's company. Rudy and Paul have proven themselves in college, at their jobs, and with their families. What happened in our growing-up years was due to circumstances that existed with my parents and those of my own doing. I believe I was also misdirected by, and had to overcome, the general belief that first-born children were the achievers, second born were not, and the youngest had it the easiest.

On the positive side, there were two breakthroughs for me in the couple years after I graduated from high school. Despite the lack of encouragement from anyone, I started going to college in the evenings. I was motivated to do well, and ended up doing so.

The other positive breakthrough came when I joined the Navy in 1951 at 20 years of age. Until then, I did not know what my actual abilities were, but I clearly found out when I took the Naval intelligence and aptitude tests. The test scores improved my self-image and confidence level. They changed my view of myself. I took a very positive stance in the Navy. I didn't knock anybody's toys over, I accelerated up the ranks with some of the highest advancement test scores in my job category. I began changing my sour grapes image into one of big, juicy red apples. The German seed started to grow deeper roots and sprout stronger branches.

My older brother Rudy used to come up with wisdoms like, "Elucidate yourself more specifically. Your dominion over comprehension is much below par." I don't know if he made it up or he read it. But I was impressed. He had other unique insights into people's behavior. He graduated fourth in his engineering class from the Illinois Institute of Technology and had a number of job offers. He chose to go with Standard Oil of Indiana, and was a success at his job until he retired. He married Rosemary and had three children, Karen, Bill, and Diane, who died in midlife of cancer.

My younger brother Paul has a master's degree in business and had a successful career as a treasury agent with the government. Since his job was considered hazardous, he was able to retire early. However, he got another job right away as an investigator with the City of Chicago and worked there the balance of years until he retired.

His wife, my sister-in-law Carol, has a doctorate degree in education. The youngest daughter, Melinda, my niece, has a doctorate degree, and the older son Derrick has advanced degrees and is a successful lawyer. Derrick married Mary and they have four children.

This ends my childhood life of growing up in Chicago during the 1930s and 1940s under the influences of the German American culture and my family's sour image, which prevailed at that time.

Chapter 11

AN INTERVIEW WITH
HERR SAUERBRATEN

T he following is a play I wrote for presentation at a party at my house for my German American friends in about 2005. It is about the Germans in America and it is presented as an interview with an older, knowledgeable German. It paints a brief, clear, and humorous picture about the history, beliefs, traits, attitudes, and culture of the German American immigrants. It covers the contributions they made to the U.S. culture and growth, from the first shipload 400 years ago to the present day.

Monica Schmidt, who conducts the interview, is a young woman journalist interested in the social history of the Germans who immigrated to America. She was born in Germany and came to the U.S. when she was nine years old. She is assigned by the local German newspaper to interview Germans on the north side of Chicago in the Lincoln/Lawrence shopping district during the Christmas season.

The first scene opens up with Monica looking around at the shoppers walking about in the shopping area. *I wonder what kind of person I'll find to interview? Oh, here comes someone.* "Excuse me, sir. I see you are shopping in the stores here in Lincoln Square, and I couldn't help seeing the German flag in your back pocket and your *Cat in the Hat* hat with 'Germany' written on the front. I'm from the local German newspaper and am interviewing some German Americans for our Christmas edition. Would you mind answering some questions?"

"Yah, yah, I vill answer your questions," he answers loudly with a German accent.

"First of all, what's your name?"

"Mein name ist Hans Sauerbraten," he states proudly.

"Oh, that's a very interesting name." She makes a screwed-up face and wonders what kind of character this guy is going to be with a name like Sauerbraten. "Are you a true German American, born in Germany, who immigrated to the United States and made it a permanent home?"

"Yah, I vass born in Germany and I haf lived here for over 50 years."

"My big question is, what have German Americans contributed to the growth and culture of the United States in comparison to other European countries? Maybe we should be looking instead at what the Italians, British, or Irish contributed as being more important than that of the Germans?" the interviewer asks.

Herr Sauerbraten snaps back, "Nein, nein don't go mit dose uder guys. Der are many goot reasons vhy you shoot be happy dat de German Americans are here in America."

"Well, okay, I'm glad to hear that. What are some of the good reasons?"

Germans Flock to U.S.

"Vell, first of all, let me give you some background information. The German Americans were here right from the beginning. The first Germans came in 1608 and lived in Jamestown, Virginia."

A crowd started to gather around the interviewer and Sauerbraten in Lincoln Square to listen to what was going on.

"Since den eight million Germans have immigrated to the U.S., the largest number of any European country. Today, including their descendents, the German Americans have over 50 million people in America, down from 60 million some years ago. They represent about one-fifth of the current 310 million plus living in the United States.

"The German Information Center talks about why they immigrated. Large groups came to the United States during the 1848 revolution in Europe. They came because they lost the revolution and the fight against oppression. They came because of hunger, pain, poverty, unemployment and terrible living conditions. They came because they saw the United States as a land of opportunity, a land of promise, a new world, and a new start. They hungered for freedom from political oppression and religious persecution. They came for better lives, land, and an abundance of food.

"In the earlier years they were processed through Ellis Island. People who had serious diseases or physical problems, criminal backgrounds, no sponsors, or had insufficient means, were sent back.

"There were different waves of German immigrants moving to the United States. Not only the original groups in the 1600s...there were large groups in the mid-1850s. They came heavily after World War I...130,000 Jews left Germany in 1939...then after World War II and in the 1950s and '60s.

"They settled down in Pennsylvania, Illinois, and Wisconsin; in other Midwestern and Rocky Mountain states, as well as many other areas of the country. Texas and California also had their communities of German Americans. Some immigrants traveled the Oregon Trail from St. Louis to California during the Gold Rush days or to Oregon in the 1800s."

Herr Sauerbraten went on, "However, it vas not all peaches and cream. Many immigrants couldn't find work right away in their trade and took menial jobs such as janitors in apartment buildings. Some immigrants who didn't have enough money to move, or didn't have an occupation or some connections, suffered in the tenement areas of New York City, in *Little Germany*."

Where Did They Come From?

"Where did the German American immigrants come from?" Monica inquired further.

"Vee come from different parts of Germany and Europe," Sauerbraten began, "not just from tiny hick towns...but from cities and town such as Munich, Bremerhaven, Berlin, Stuttgart, Dresden, Frankfurt, and Hannover...vee come from different states such as Bavaria, Bremen, Schwabia, and Schleswig-Holstein. Some of us come from parts of other countries that used to be part of Germany, such as the Danzig Corridor in Poland on the North Sea; and Pomerania, south of the Baltic Sea, which was divided up between Germany and Poland. Am I throwing too much out too fast?" Sauerbraten asked.

"No, I can get it all down," Monica answered.

"They also came from other parts of Europe that used to be part of Germany but switched hands; the Sudenland in Czechoslovakia, Alsace Lorraine in France, and Donauschwabia, which was mostly in Hungary along the Danube River."

And Herr Sauerbraten added, "Die schweine hunde von France and England took some of these areas away from Germany after the First World War."

"Now, don't be nasty, Mr. *Sauerkraut*," the interviewer warned.

"Hey, dummkopf," Hans snapped back, "my name is SAUERBRATEN, nicht Sauerkraut."

"Now, now, Herr Sauerbraten, where is your Christmas spirit?" Monica retorted.

Left Wonderful Homeland

Herr Sauerbraten settled himself and went on. The crowd standing around listening got bigger. "Vee left our beautiful green country in central Europe, the land of Bismark, Hindenburg, and Kaiser Wilhelm. The land of Martin Luther, who started the Protestant religion; and Gutenberg, the inventor of typesetting for books. The land of Max Schmeling, a German prize fighter who won the world's heavy weight championship in the 1930s, and then he lost it to Joe Louis." Sauerbraten added a comment, "Schmeling vould have never lost dat fight if Louis didn't fight dirty."

"Well, that's your opinion, Mr. *Sauerpuss*, but please go on with your story."

"Mein nam ist Sauerbraten, nicht Sauerpuss," Hans complained. "But I vill go on even though you call me funny names. Vee left our homeland of the Messerschmitt, Stuka, and rockets. Vee left the industrious design and production quality of cars such as the Mercedes, BMW, and Volkswagens. The superior manufacturing gave the world vunderbar cameras, instruments, and machines."

How Did They Get Here?

Monica continued her interview. "Fine, the Germans' industrial machine is great, but let's get off of that. How did the German immigrants get here from Germany?"

"Vee mostly came on ships such as the *Bremen*, *Gripsholm*, *Europe*, and *Berlin* in the 1800s and first half of the 1900s. The wave of German immigrants who came later in the 1950s and '60s came either by ship or airplanes. Most of us had to take trains from New York to wherever we were going. They sailed from Bremerhaven and Rotterdam, were jam-packed in small ships and suffered terrible conditions. Some died on the voyage coming here.

"In earlier years the immigrants had to go through Ellis Island in New York. If they didn't meet the health standards for immigrants, or the requirements of having some money and a sponsor who would be responsible for them, they would be sent back to Germany."

Lifestyles

Monica responded, "Well, Mr. Sauerbraten, you sure know a lot about the history of the German Americans. There are more questions I want to ask you if you don't mind. You could be a big help for this article."

"Ja, I am the history guy in our German club," Herr Sauerbraten proudly exclaimed.

"What about the lifestyles of the German Americans in the U.S.?" Monica asked.

"They like to keep a lot of their Old World traditions. Many groups have their own schools and churches. They love to sing in choral groups and have their own singing clubs, such as the Rheinischer Gesang Verein Singing Club in the Chicago area," Herr Sauerbraten answered. "There are numerous German soccer clubs in the U.S. There are many German social clubs that meet monthly, have special dinners and entertainment, and celebrate holidays together. They prefer German food. There used to be many German restaurants, which have largely disappeared in recent years. They love their beer."

The crowd grew more and Sauerbraten looked around as he spoke and beamed. He was in his glory.

Beliefs

Monica continued to make her notes and went on with the following question: "What are some of the beliefs of the German Americans?"

Sauerbraten answered after some thought. "The German Americans have many strong beliefs that…it's a sin to be late for work, for an appointment, or for visiting people; you should work hard every minute of the time at your job. They feel guilty when they are not working; do it right the first time; you should not be a sleepyhead and get up late. It's a sin to throw food away. You should see how clean der plates are. Families and self-discipline are very important in their lives…neatness and cleanliness are supremely important…you should always try to be perfect. Day don't beleef in slavery. We need some of that stuff around here in today's world. And, mein Gott, day are a proud bunch!"

German Day Picnics

Herr Sauerbraten went on, "German Americans celebrated German Day every summer in the 1930s and '40s in Harms Park on the north side of Chicago on Western Avenue. It occupied most of the city block and had a high wood wall around it. An entrance fee was required. People came early in the day on German Day. Families and friends settled down on picnic tables and stayed there the whole day. The children scampered off and ran amuck in the park and would not be seen again except to eat and when it was time to go home. They came back to their picnic table dirty and sweaty.

"Most families brought their own food, bratwurst, bockwurst, sauerkraut, smoked pork chops, and potatoes, and cooked on open fires. They brought German-type black bread, real butter, liver sausage and other cold cuts. Others bought their food at the food stands. German bands played oompa music and polkas and people hopped around the dance floor for hours. Some German women wore colorful, fluffy Dirdnl dresses from the Bavarian Mountain region in Germany, and some men wore the Bavarian leather pants and jackets, plus Bavarian hats with a feather in them. German club officers and local politician made speeches.

"One big feature of Harms Park was the gigantic wooden boat swings that swung back and forth high in the air. It was the only ride in the park and kids rode it over and over. Kids participated in games and races. A highlight of the German Day picnic was the parade with groups and floats from various German clubs, and the feature float with the newly chosen Prince and Princess."

Occupations

"What were the occupations of the typical immigrant?" Monica asked.

"The immigrants who came here included machinists, tool and die makers, carpenters, cabinet makers, farmers, and unskilled workers looking for a better life and opportunities to work. Many of us made a lot of money in the United States either by working long hours or going into businesses. Vee beat out de dummkopf Americans in the skilled trades."

"Now stop that," the interviewer complained to Sauerbraten.

"Those aren't things we want to say in the paper. I would appreciate it if you didn't make those statements."

"Yah, yah. Wie du villst."

"And stop talking German."

"A very interesting ting about these skilled craftsmen who immigrated to America from Germany, dat most people don't tink about, is that they were the backbone of the mighty U.S. production of war equipment. Day vere the backbone of skilled machinists, tool and die makers, and welders of airplanes, ships, and guns that helped defeat Germany in the Second World War. At one time America was producing 1,000 planes a month, and dozens of ships, due in large part to German American craftsmanship.

"And the American-born sons and grandsons were right alongside of them, many as engineers. The point here is that many German Americans had relatives and friends yet in Germany during the war. The skills and industry of the German Americans in the production of war equipment ended up posing a danger to their loved ones. However, the loyalty of most of them was to the United States, and they hoped that what they did didn't affect their loved ones still in Germany."

Famous German Americans and Their Descendents

"That's very interesting, Mr. Sauerbraten. Please go on. Give me some more reasons why America should be happy you guys are here. Who were some of the famous people that came here from Germany?"

"Vell..." Herr Sauerbraten thought a bit. "Most of the first beer brewers, Miller, Pabst, Schlitz, Stroh, Anheuser/Busch, and Coors came from Germany. There are movie stars, Marlene Dietrich, Elka Summer mit die nice boobs, and Maximillion Schell, to name a few. German intellectuals who immigrated here made contributions to the country and excelled in art, science, architecture, industry, entertainment, theology, government, and the military.

"You vouldn't haf had the help of the world's most famous scientist, Albert Einstein. And Werner von Braun and his crew of rocket engineers, who were crucial in the U.S.'s development of the rockets to the moon. Mies Van Der Rohe, der architech who vass right here in Chicago and designed some modern buildings in downtown Chicago and the school buildings at the Illinois Institute of Technology. Walter Gropius and Helmut Jahn are two more German architects."

People in the crowd nodded and mumbled, "I didn't know that."

"Dos var really schmardt guys, not like some dummkopfs..."

"Don't say any more, Mr. Sauerbraten, or your name will be *Wienerschnitzel* in the article."

"Den der vas die children of dies schmardt German Americans who were born in America of German parents: President Eisenhower, a leader in winning World War II against Germany, as well as a popular, two-term president; Oscar Mayer, der viener guy; Heinz, mit der 57 different tings in jars; George Eastman, mit der Kodak cameras; J. Robert Oppenheimer, who ran the making of the atomic bomb in Los Alamos during the Second World War, was a German descendent.

"Der vas famous writers who were German American descendents, like John Steinbeck, Carl Sandburg, Theodore Dreiser, Walter Lippman, H.L. Mencken, Joseph Pulitzer, Kurt Vonnegut, Geisel (author of Dr. Seuss), Charles Schultz (author of the comic strip 'Peanuts'). Plus der vas movies stars that were of German descent...Doris Day, Sandra Bullock, Leonardo DiCaprio, Clark Gable, Bruce Willis, and Rene Zellweger are a few. In music there was Oscar Hammerstein, Elvis Presley, Lawrence Welk, Bruno Walter, and Wurlizer. In sports der vas Johnny Weissmuller, Babe Ruth, and Casey Stengel."

"Okay, now you are really coming up with something that puts the German Americans ahead of other countries."

Contributions to Our Culture

Herr Sauerbraten continued, "Da Germans brought with them two of the most beautiful Christmas songs in the world, 'Silent Night' and 'Oh, Tannenbaum,' which in English you know as 'Oh, Christmas Tree.' I really like singing it." Hans starts to sing, "Oh, Tannenbaum, oh, Tannenbaum, vee green sind deine blaette…"

Some people in the crowd sang with him and more shoppers gathered around to see what the commotion was.

Monica cut Sauerbraten off. "Let's go on with the contributions to our culture...save the singing."

"Ja, ja! Da Germans also gave America two wonderful traditions, the Christmas tree and Santa Claus. But da Christmas tree tradition in Germany is different than in the United States. Most families wait until Christmas Eve to put up their tree. While the father puts up a live tree and decorates it in the living room, the children have to stay in another room. He puts real candles on the tree, instead of light bulbs, and lights them with a match. Then they all go in the living room to see the tree and exchange presents."

German Foods and Words Introduced to Americans

"What are some German foods and words introduced to America by the German immigrants over the years?" Monica asked.

"Oh, dat's an easy one," Sauerbraten responded. "Some of the foods they introduced to this country were also words that were absorbed into the English language. Think of frankfurter, bratwurst, beer, pretzel, sauerkraut, sauerbraten, roladen, und apple strudel. Additional words absorbed were gesundheit, waltz, angst, dumm-kopf, and auf wiedersehen."

Pulling It All Together

"Okaaay…" Monica broke in, "that sounds really good to me and I think I have enough for the article. You have been an encyclopedia of knowledge about the German Americans. But, could you give us one last statement for our readers about the German Americans that pulls it all together?"

"Yah..." Hans gave this some thought. "It vass a beautiful, mutually beneficial relationship. The Germans have had a great and prosperous life in America. They have enjoyed the freedoms of America. But they still luff der motherland even as Americans. They still have lingering visions of der *mutterland*—where the sky is bluer, the grass greener, and the apples bigger. But America also owes them a lot, too, for what they have contributed to the culture and growth of the country. I think the German immigrants helped America to grow into a better and stronger country."

"Thank you very much, Mr. Bratwurst...no, I'm sorry, I mean...Mr. Sauerbraten! Your interview will be in the Christmas edition of our German newspaper next week. Have a Merry Christmas!"

The crowd applauded.

"Danke schoen, and same to you, Fraulein Schmidt! Ach...look at all the people who have gathered around us." He addressed the crowd. "Vhy don't vee all sing 'Silent Night' together."

And so they did, led by Sauerbraten, who sang it in German. The interviewer listened and looked at Sauerbraten with a feeling of admiration and amazement.

Part III

THE ROOTS AND BRANCHES SPROUT OUT

Chapter 12
LANDLUBBER SAILOR

From the Great Lakes to California to the Aleutian Islands

On my first day of recruit training in October 1955 at the Naval Training Center north of Chicago, I faced what could have been a disastrous encounter. All of the recruits were in our assigned barracks carrying our heavy sea bags to our bunks down a narrow aisle of the building. The bags were filled with our new Navy uniforms and other gear. There were 20 bunk beds on the left and right sides as you entered in the center of the building, enough for a company of 80 recruits. In the middle of the barracks there was a common area for letter writing and socializing.

Another recruit was walking to a bunk bed farther down and accidently bumped into me, almost knocking me over. I whipped around and indignantly yelled at him, "What the hell is wrong with you?"

He glared at me. "Are you looking for trouble, you jerk?" he said in a menacing tone. He wasn't much bigger than me but he was trim and all muscle. He grabbed me by my shirt collar and was ready to smash my face in. He looked ferocious.

"Wait...hold on, Tony!" A buddy of his held him back and warned him, "If you hit him, you'll be in big trouble. It can goof up your time in the Navy."

Tony's fist was still clenched and he was anxious to throw a knockout punch.

I got nervous and scared. I didn't expect this. "Take it easy...I didn't really mean anything...I'm really sorry," I pleaded. I kept up with the apologies. "I'm sorry...I'm sorry!"

He started to simmer down, relaxed his grip on my shirt, and unclenched his fist.

His friend pleaded, "Let him go, he didn't mean anything."

"Okay, but watch what you're saying, punk," he warned me arrogantly and turned to go back to carrying his sea bag to his bunk.

I found out later why his friend told him to take it easy. He was a champion Golden Gloves boxer from Chicago and he had plans to get on a Navy boxing team. I'm glad he didn't make his boxing exhibition with me as the guinea pig.

One might wonder why I decided to join the Navy at that time. It was in the early '50s and the Korean War was raging. Any guy turning 20 years old was eligible for being drafted into the Army for two years and he had to register for the draft. However, if he was going to college he could be deferred until he graduated. Also, he could avoid being drafted into the Army and risking foot soldier combat duty in Korea by joining the Navy or Air Force for four years, as long as he signed up within 90 days after his 20th birthday. That is just what my two school friends, Dave and Herb, did. Their 20th birthdays were both in January. They had already joined the Navy, and were gone and on duty. We could also avoid being drafted into the Army by joining the Marines for two years, as my friend Bill did.

My 20th birthday was coming up in July 1951, at which time I had to go in for a physical. I was okay, classified 1A, physically qualified for military duty. There was time to make up my mind, so I let a couple of months go by. I made the same decision as my friends and joined the Navy.

I signed up in the Navy, took a basic qualification test in the Naval enlistment office near downtown Chicago, passed and was accepted. I was inducted into the Navy, sworn in on Halloween day, October 31st, 1951 in the recruiting office. They sent me and a group of other guys by train to the Great Lakes Naval Training Center. Upon arrival they gave us an orientation speech about life in the Navy, obeying military rules, and information on the layout of the boot camp. We were assigned to a company and to our barracks, and taken over by our chief petty officer, who was in charge of us. The next day we were outfitted with uniforms and we had the hair on our heads shaved off. This, unfortunately, identified us as new skinheads, a form of lowlife in the Navy. We received our metal identification tags with our service numbers (mine was 304 79 78) and blood type stamped on them, and we were instructed to wear the chain around our necks at all times.

After a couple of days of preliminaries, the episode with Mr. Golden Gloves guy, and being outfitted with uniforms, we were ready to march to the mess hall together as a company. It was late afternoon and time for dinner. The weather was cold and blustery in the Chicago area. An early snowfall was blowing around and the wind chill was giving our bald heads the shivers. We were instructed to put our new P-coats on and then all 80 apprentice seamen in our company assembled into a marching group and proceeded on to the mess hall. We found that several other boot training companies were already ahead of us in line standing outside. We stood outside behind them in the icy Lake Michigan wind and snow, shivering for maybe 45 minutes before we got inside the mess hall and ate dinner.

Damn! What a start. Regrets of having joined the Navy already started and set in before the end of the second day. Maybe being a foot soldier in Korea wouldn't have been so bad. Here we were with no hats on our hairless heads, freezing, scared to death with threats about what would happen if we didn't obey all superiors and military rules, and the horrors of the stockade.

And to add to the shock of this new, strange way of living, a third upsetting thing happened the first night. A group of Naval military police barged into our barracks around midnight, like today's SWAT squads, and arrested a few recruits that were involved with drugs. I don't think many of us slept much that first night. Then we were rudely awakened at 5:30 a.m. with a recorded bugle call and banging of garbage can covers. It was enough to crush the brain of any young guy during the start of his service.

The recruit training in 1951 involved marching everywhere with the company of 80 guys—to classes in seamanship, gunnery, fire control, swimming, and rules of military conduct. The rest of the remaining free time was spent in large part washing clothes, polishing shoes with a so-called "spit shine," and writing home. If there was any more free time it was spent complaining about the Navy, about being a recruit, saluting officers, and stuff like that.

We had to take a barrage of IQ and aptitude tests during the first week. The test scores were used as a basis for assignments to an appropriate job category, for assignments to specialty schools, or for assignments to a duty station after graduation from recruit training.

Luckily, much to my surprise and contrary to the opinions of some of my family members, the tests showed my mental ability and aptitude scores ranked quite high, being in the upper third of all Naval personnel. I was immediately encouraged and more optimistic about my future. *Hey*, I thought, *I may not have to sling hamburgers all my life as my family had me believing.*

The test scores not only bolstered my ego, self-image, and confidence, they also made me eligible to pursue one of three options besides being an enlisted man. I could become a Navy pilot, go to four years of free college in the NROTC, or go to the 90-day Officers Training School. Sure, I would become an officer, but I would also have to spend several extra years of full-time duty thereafter, and maybe eight years as a reserve officer. This didn't appeal to me at all. Also, I chose not to fly planes off carrier decks, attend college, or be a 90-day wonder. I chose just to serve out my enlistment of four years as an enlisted man.

There were three Recruit Naval Training Centers (RNTCs) in the United States at the time; one in the Great Lakes, one in San Diego, and another in Norfolk, VA. Today there is only one left, a centralized and expanded facility in Great Lakes. Both San Diego and Norfolk no longer train recruits.

After about eight weeks of exhaustive recruit training and the bashing of our egos, it finally ended. I graduated and received a week's leave or so to go home and parade in front of my parents, relatives, and friends in my uniform. I was no longer a lowly recruit with two short yellow stripes on my upper sleeve, but now had three white stripes to signify I was advanced to seaman.

I'm in the third row from the bottom, third guy from the right.

After boot training was over I was assigned to the Naval Security Group as a Communications Technician. I really didn't know what the heck I would be doing at that time. It was very secretive. The FBI made a security background check on my parents, as well as me, while I was going through the eight weeks of basic training. I ended up with a top-secret clearance rating.

The first phase in the advanced training required of this job was to go to the San Diego Radio School, which was about eight weeks long. We would learn and practice receiving and sending the Morse Code. "DashDashDash—DotDotDot—DashDashDash" is the code for SOS. Some of us could catch on and read and send the code fast enough and others stumbled along through endless practice sessions.

You either had it or you didn't. I was in the middle, but didn't do well enough to continue going in that direction.

After the eight weeks of Morse Code schooling and separating radio people from teletype people out, my next school assignment was Imperial Beach, California for further specialized communications training. This rather small Naval facility was along the California coastline a few miles from the Mexican border and Tijuana. It looked more like a vacation resort. Many of the instructors lived there with their wives and children on the base.

We received further, in-depth training in specialized communications involving teletype networks and equipment. We were also blessed with several WAVES (Women Accepted for Volunteer Emergency Service), who were also in training. The instructors tempered their language and treatment in the classes because of the WAVES students.

We got enough time off and could leave the base for sightseeing. You could go to Tijuana, Mexico or to San Diego and visit places like La Jolla or Coronado Island. You could go to Los Angeles and go sightseeing to the Hollywood Bowl, Grumman's Chinese Theater, or Universal Studios and more. Some guys got messed up in Tijuana by drinking too much and fooling around with women they met at the bars. Some brought back bed bugs or sexual diseases, and others found themselves in a Mexican jail for a day or two.

The schooling at Imperial Beach, on the teletype side of our job, took about four months. This ended our training in this category of work, and we were then sent to regular duty stations. It so happened that in our specialty rate we primarily worked only in onshore communication stations, and not on ships. We were landlubbers, not sea-going sailors, we found out.

Herb sent for duty to Alaska, to Adak in the Aleutian Islands for a year. 1953

Trees don't grow well on Adak, only tundra grass.

Of the dozen or so communications shore stations around the U.S. and world I was assigned to Adak, Alaska, an island near the end of the string of Aleutian Islands. It was barren; no trees, some tundra grass, and a lot of husky dogs. It wasn't very cold there, but you spent most of your time inside working, watching Hollywood movies, occasional U.S.O. shows, drinking in the beer hall for a couple of hours at night, and sleeping. There was no place to go and nothing to do outside on Adak.

The only excitement that happened was one night when I was standing in the hallway talking to buddies. We heard a rumble that got louder and louder as it approached. The walls and the floors vibrated. Then there was a jolt that lifted me about six inches off the floor. We wondered what had happened. Later we found out it was a six-point earthquake caused by an underwater eruption, and that our island of Adak was standing on two thin underwater pinnacles. The barracks we were in didn't collapse or fall apart because they were built with double thick reinforced concrete foundations and walls to withstand earthquakes.

With buddies in the beer hall making our own spaghetti dinner

It was a boring, endless year on this little island in the Aleutians, but fortunately they didn't make you stay there more than a year, as with better stations that have two-year tours of duty. When the year ended in late fall I was overjoyed at leaving it, and looked forward to being home for the Christmas holidays, then moving on to Germany.

Chapter 13
MEETING MY WIFE
AND
HASSLES IN GERMANY, 1954

As I previously mentioned, I was never assigned to do duty aboard a ship during the four years I was in the Navy, only to land communications stations in different parts of the world, such as Alaska, Germany, and London.

After leaving Adak in the Aleutian Islands in the fall of 1953, I was transferred to a communication station in Bremerhaven, Germany. But first I was able to go home for Christmas to be with my family in Chicago. Over two years of my four-year enlistment were over. I was at my halfway point.

Early in January 1954, per my transfer papers, I flew to New York to the Brooklyn Navy Yard for boarding on a transport ship to Germany as a passenger. However, my transport ship wasn't due to leave for two weeks, so on the nights off at the Naval facility I took the subway train from the Brooklyn Navy Yard to Manhattan.

I went to see several smash Broadway plays while in New York... *The Seven Year Itch* with Tom Ewell, *The King of Siam* with Yul Brenner, *Inherit the Wind* with Melvyn Douglas. All were made into popular movies later. I also did some sightseeing; Times Square, the Empire State Building, the United Nations, the Bowery, and Columbus Park.

Most of the military passengers aboard the ship, which was sailing to Bremerhaven, were U.S. soldiers going for duty somewhere in Germany. At that time we occupied a number of areas there after the end of World War II. Bremerhaven was on the northern coast of

Germany and bordered the North Sea. It was the main port for ship arrivals and departures in Germany. From there, soldiers who were assigned to duty in Germany took a train to their final destination, which was usually in central Germany, such as Stuttgart or Karlsruhe.

When the two weeks were over at the Brooklyn Navy Yard I boarded the ship. The people manning the transport ship were Merchant Marine sailors. So, being a sailor, they gave me a job typing for the second in command of the ship, the Executive Officer. I went to his office the first morning out to sea and the commander gave me some typing to do. I sat there for a few hours feeling sicker and sicker by the minute. The letters being typed on the paper began swirling about, and I felt I was about to barf all over the typewriter. I told the commander that I felt seasick. He told me to go to the sickbay. I went and after that I lay in my bunk bed for the rest of the voyage. I couldn't go into the mess hall to eat or get up without getting dizzy. Instead, I bought a bunch of Clark candy bars, which I ate for the next four or five days in my bunk bed and never got completely over the seasickness.

I was really happy and excited to be assigned to the communication station in Bremerhaven. I would be able to stay there to the end of my four-year enlistment, for almost two more years. My mother, who was born in Germany and immigrated to United States in 1927, was also excited about it. It just so happened that she had lived in Bremerhaven for some years before immigrating here. Before I went to Germany she contacted old friends of hers in Bremerhaven and told them I was coming. They wrote my mother back and said I was more than welcome to visit them at any time. It was nice to know there were friends that I could visit there.

Once I arrived I couldn't visit them right away, because during a basic medical indoctrination I fainted after getting a blood test. I fell on the concrete steps in the basement of a medical building, which resulted in a big, unsightly bruise on the side of my face. A week or two later, when the bruise didn't look so bad, I decided to visit them. I hopped into a German taxi outside the German Navy barracks, which we occupied, and told the taxi driver, "Post Strasse Zwoelf bitte." He zipped down the confusing streets like he was on a racetrack and was there in no time.

I went up to their second-story apartment and turned the bell in the middle of the door. My future wife opened the door. There she was, dressed warmly for the colder apartment conditions in Germany, with a wool sweater and skirt. She greeted me, invited me in, and introduced me to her parents. We had dinner later and we worked hard at making ourselves understood. Hanna's father, Ewald, said I was welcome for dinner anytime. Ewald, and Hanna's mother, Luise, were both gracious, friendly, and humble people.

Hanna's sister, Annegret, who is younger by two years than Hanna, wasn't there because she had immigrated to the U.S. a year or two earlier, having been sponsored by an aunt in the Chicago area.

I was on a three-day communication work cycle in Bremerhaven and every third day I went to visit them and have dinner with them. Hanna's father told her to take me around town and show me things like the zoo, the beach, and the old ships in the harbor, which she did. Her parents were very generous and kind.

Ewald worked at the city theater as a tailor and he got two free show tickets every two weeks. I told them I would be interested in seeing some plays or operettas, so Hanna and I started seeing the shows together. One play we saw was *Anna Lucasta*, starring Eartha Kitt. For those who are not familiar with her, she was a legendary performer with many Emmy and Tony awards, an American and international multi-lingual singer and actress. *Lucasta* is a sad story of a black prostitute who tries to leave her past behind. Hanna and I both loved the theater, and not only enjoyed the programs, but also being together. Romance blossomed and we fell in love.

Herb and Hanna in Bremerhaven, Germany in 1954

My wife lived on the second floor of this
apartment building in Bremerhaven.

Hanna's parents, Luise and Ewald, enjoying ritual
afternoon coffee and cake

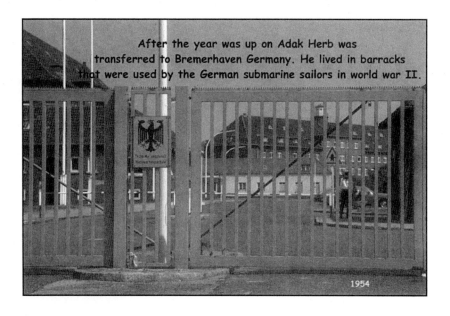

After the year was up on Adak Herb was
transferred to Bremerhaven Germany. He lived in barracks
that were used by the German submarine sailors in world war II.

1954

I had enough knowledge of the German language and an ear for the sounds from my parents and German classes in high school and college. Hence, I was able to get by communicating with Hanna and her parents, plus I could make myself understood. I kept a small red English/German pocket dictionary with me for when we got stuck. We only spoke German, no English, and I quickly picked up local expressions and words and learned how to pronounce words fairly well.

Hanna was just the opposite of what the American image was of a German woman, often stereotyped as stout, muscular, a big blond with pigtails, and carrying a bunch of beer steins in each hand. She was rather short, slim, petite, with an engaging smile, which followed the characteristics of her father.

My wife and her sister with their mother in 1943,
when they still had their pigtails.

Hanna and I visited her aunts and uncles, who seemed to be all over the place in Bremerhaven. Most of the time we would be served cake and strong coffee, and afterwards a schnapps and a beer or liquors.

Hanna worked in a small wholesale tobacco business in Bremerhaven as a bookkeeper. She had gone to school until she was 14 years old and then served a three-year apprenticeship as a bookkeeper. In addition to the wholesale sales and distribution, the tobacco business sold cigarettes and cigars retail over the counter. German cigarettes were sold in packages of 10, instead of in 20s as the American brands. The German cigarettes didn't taste all that good, and the American cigarettes were preferred by most Germans. Hence, there was a black market for American cigarettes after the war which lasted for 10 years or so.

Black Market Cigarettes

I was smoking heavily at the time, about 30 cigarettes a day. It was an era where it was popular to smoke, but I decided to give it up. I had misgivings about smoking. My fingers were stained with nicotine. I would be brushing my teeth in the morning and taking drags on a cigarette at the same time. I coughed from the smoking. Food didn't taste as good anymore. The last thing I did before I went to sleep at night was to smoke a cigarette. I had to constantly see that I had a package of cigarettes with me as well as matches or a lighter. I also had to have an ash tray around when we were inside.

Luckily, I happened to read an abbreviated version of *How to Quit Smoking* in the *Reader's Digest*. I closely followed the self-help guide on how to do so and was able to quit in a few months. Details on the process of quitting are described in a previous chapter, "Mischievous Shenanigans."

As a result of the black market, we had an embarrassing situation involving Hanna's father. He was a confirmed smoker and liked the American cigarettes, especially one of the favorite brands, Camels, during these years. American servicemen in Germany were allowed to buy one carton of cigarettes a week at the PX or commissary. Since Hanna's father liked the American cigarettes and he was so kind and generous to me, I bought my weekly allotment and gave them to him. I would bring them over in a brown American grocery store bag. After about four or five months the cartons accumulated, because he was only smoking about a few packs a week. He stuffed the extra cartons into dresser drawers, kitchen cabinets, and so on to keep them out of sight.

Then one day the German police banged on his door and demanded to be let in. "We know you have been getting black market cigarettes and haven't been reporting them or paying the import taxes on them. We know you have them, so don't try and deny it."

Hanna's father's heart sank to the floor. He never really did anything wrong in his whole life, and was a law abiding, humble man. The police started to ransack the apartment. They opened all the dresser drawers and pulled the cartons of Camels and Lucky Strikes out. They went through the wardrobe cabinets, which the Germans used because they didn't have any closets. They searched the kitchen cabinets and found cartons everywhere. When they were satisfied, they tallied up how many cigarettes there were. "We will first calculate how many cartons you got in the last five months on the black market. We will then multiply the rate of import taxes by the number of cartons and add interest for being late in paying import taxes on them. You have to come with us to the police station and we will file the charges and fill out the paperwork."

Unfortunately, the police were driving scooters with sidecars where passengers could sit. Hanna's father had to ride sitting in the sidecar, exposed to the public. Neighbors and friends who happened to be around at the time saw him being hauled away through town. It was a deep, shameful experience for him and a blot on an honest man's record in life.

Later, we surmised how they found out about the contraband I was bringing. Two old women who ran a small grocery store on the first floor of their apartment building must have been peeking out of the window at times when I came with the American grocery bags. It was a dead giveaway and we believed they reported it to the police. They were either jealous or good citizens. In any case, they weren't very friendly neighbors, if it was them.

Otherwise these were idyllic days for us in the spring and summer of 1954. We not only saw the plays, but went to the movies and saw *Gone with the Wind* with German dubbed in. It sounded strange to my ears. We went to the beautiful parks in town on Sunday afternoons; one was Burger Park and the other Speckenbutal.

There were day trips. One was a bus trip to the Alten Land (old country) along the Weser River where we saw the fruit trees blossoming in spring. From there we took a tour boat farther down the river to Hamburg and the Reperbahn Park, which was right on the river.

We also took a longer trip to the Munich area in southern Germany to visit my stepfather's family, the Bierlings and the Oels. They were so gracious and so much fun to be with that we became lifelong friends with them. At first it was just Josef and Gertraud and her mother. In later years, we have gone back there many times by plane from Chicago and visited them and the two Oel boys, Hans and Werner, who were kids back then. After they were grown up, married, and had kids, we visited Hans Oel and family in the Ausburg area, and they and their children have visited us in Chicago. They are a wonderful family and we are proud to know them.

After about three or four months of courtship and falling in love, Hanna and I decided to get engaged. The typical German engagement ring in those days was a plain gold band, with both the man and woman wearing it, first on the left hand during the engagement and then moving it to the right hand after they were married. It was very economical. There was no separate diamond wedding ring for the woman. We planned to be married in June of the next year, 1955, a few months before I was to be discharged later in October, when my four-year enlistment would be over.

Then, just when we thought everything was going so smoothly, I was notified that in November of 1954 I would be transferred to London. It shocked us both and we wondered what would happen with our marriage plans.

Chapter 14

LIFE IN LONDON

Marriage Approval Delayed

When the orders came in to transfer me to London, I requested to stay in Bremerhaven at my current duty station. I explained to the Naval personnel the reason I wanted to stay there. I said I was engaged to someone there and planned to marry the following June. That was the exact wrong thing to tell them since I was in a classified work group and wasn't really supposed to "patronize with German nationals," as they put it. They said you are going, and I went.

The group of us who were being transferred from Bremerhaven to London boarded a plane and flew from Germany to London. We then took a train from the military Air Force base on the outskirts of London to the "tube" subway system. We road the underground transit to Grosvenor's Square, which was occupied by numerous American facilities—the American Embassy for one; and by the American Chief of Naval Operations in Europe, CINCNELM for another, where we were assigned. Further, the square consisted of other military and U.S. agency buildings, and medical facilities for American servicemen and embassy personnel.

We checked in at the CINCNELM office building and received instructions on living in London and working in the Naval Security communication facilities.

There were no barracks in London for U.S. Naval personnel. You had to find a room or flat to rent for yourself in town and they gave you subsistence pay for the rent and for food. From a list of possible rentals I found a place on Oxford Street near Hyde Park, a studio flat that I shared with a regular Navy career man close to his 20-year retirement point. I could easily walk from the flat to the CINCNELM building in Grosvenor's Square.

London was wonderful. The Navy personnel at the CINCNELM building were given Wednesday afternoons off to do cultural sightseeing. I took advantage of this, either on Wednesdays and on days off, and saw Trafalgar Square, Piccadilly Circus, Buckingham Palace, the Towers of London, Westminster Abbey, Big Ben, the Houses of Parliament, and St. James. I shopped at Selfridge's Department Store on Oxford Street, which was a tourist attraction. Living in the central area of London, you could walk to Piccadilly, to theaters with the latest movies, and to stage plays.

I enjoyed listening to the BBC on the radio, to the sophisticated way the English spoke the language and the cultural programs they put on. I read the London newspapers and enrolled in a seven-lesson home study course on better conversation. I think it cost a few pounds. They taught you to stick with the subject, not jump around too much, avoid controversial subjects, pick out interesting topics to talk about which stimulate interest, improve your vocabulary, and more.

Some serious problems popped up regarding my marriage plans, which could have completely goofed things up. I made a mistake and told some of the guys I worked with about wanting to get married to a German woman in Bremerhaven and that I was disappointed at being transferred to London. Somehow my supervisor in our communication's office misinterpreted what I said, and reported that he thought I was planning to go AWOL and back to Germany. In fact, he recommended as a solution that I be transferred to Port Lyauty, a communication station in northern Africa. He completely distorted the situation and got the commander of our unit to start the transfer process.

Hence, I was called into the commander's office and questioned. He started off with, "The reason I called you in here is that I've got a report that you might go AWOL and go back to Germany to a girlfriend."

I looked incredulously at him. My thoughts were, *That's ridiculous.* There may be some kooks in the Navy that would do this, but I certainly was not one. I looked him straight in the eye and answered, "I assure you, sir, I have no such intentions. It's true that I am engaged to someone in Bremerhaven and we are planning to get married. But I know her family...also my mother came from Bremerhaven and she knows the family. This isn't the normal situation of a G.I. going goofy over some girl. I have an absolutely clean record. I would never do something like that. I plan to go through regular Navy channels to request approval for the marriage."

Just then I saw the officer that my supervisor, Moore, reported to at another desk on the other side of the office. The commander saw I was looking at him. I nodded over to where he was, frowned, and said, "I think this is something Moore and the Lt. Commander have cooked up."

The commander understood what I meant and believed it. He stared down at the report papers in front of him for a minute or two, and apparently was evaluating the situation. "You're okay, Wendes. I'll put a stop to this transfer. I see the situation is not what the report indicates." He went on to warn me there had been bad marriage situations that occurred between American servicemen and German and English women, and to be careful.

I was allowed to process my request to get married, filling out lengthy military forms with all the required information. Hanna's family would be investigated for security purposes. Getting married under these conditions in Europe in the 1950s after the war was a hassle, especially if you were a U.S. citizen in a security group, a serviceman with a top-secret clearance, and were marrying a German citizen. The military viewed this as a security risk.

There were delays and complications on getting the marriage approval from the Navy. I waited for a couple of months before inquiring in the Naval personnel office about the status of the approval. "Nothing yet. Wait a month or two yet." It went on from the end of 1954, and several months into 1955.

We had scheduled the wedding for June 18th and it was getting stressfully closer. Not only was my mother in Chicago booking a flight to come to the wedding, but there were bureaucratic forms and things to get taken care of with the German government in order to get married, just about as bad as military red tape. I had to make arrangements for my flight from London to Germany. Reservations for our honeymoon had to be made. We needed a car rental. What if they refused to let me get married? What a mess it would be!

I continued to make all the arrangements, assuming the marriage would get approved early enough. When I inquired in April, they tracked down the paperwork that was in progress, but had no idea when it would come through. I could also be disapproved yet. At this point I decided to get some help. I asked a chief petty officer I worked with, who had some contacts in the personnel department, to see what he could do to get the process expedited.

The final approval came in May, about one month before the scheduled wedding. Hooray! I was happy we finally got the approval. But…I was notified I would be transferred out of the top-secret security group I was in, have a lower security clearance, and I would be transferred to another office in London accordingly. It didn't matter that much to me since I was not making a career of the Navy and would soon be discharged.

Chapter 15

THE WEDDING; A BUMPY ROAD
ON OUR HONEYMOON

I applied for and got a 10-day leave from my Navy duties in London for my wedding and honeymoon, and flew to Bremerhaven early to have some time to finalize things before the wedding. My mother arrived from Chicago a couple of days early, also. Then, Hanna's mother and my mother went with Hanna and me to the Standes Amp (city hall) to get the German government's legal marriage papers. Hanna was also busy with her wedding dress, the bridesmaids, flowers, and the church arrangements.

A tradition in Bremerhaven, on the eve before the wedding, was that friends and relatives came and smashed dishes on the sidewalk in front of your house. The wedding party, aunts and uncles, and our mothers had the fun of the throwing and smashing of the dishes. It's called Polter Abend in German, and means "wedding eve." Tradition has it that the bride and groom then have to clean it all up. So we were given brooms and dust pans and went to work. Afterwards, we had a small party at Hanna's apartment and everybody got happy.

We were married in the Alte Kirche (Old Church), an Evangelical Lutheran church from the reformation, around the corner from Hanna's house on Post Strasse, on June 18, 1955. The church was built in the 1500s and still was in good shape. Dark, shiny wood trim, carved statues, and pews decorated the interior and had a look of elegance. It was not a large church, seating only about 100 people.

The organ started playing and three little children—Ilka and Gert, who were a brother and sister, and another neighborhood girl— walked up the center aisle. Ilka carried the wedding veil, the other two children threw flowers.

Hanna had four bridesmaids. Two of them were her cousins, Kathi and Marriane, but I didn't have a best man because that was not a German custom. The bridesmaids, in their attractive dresses, and their partners, in black suits, walked up the aisle, and then stood on each side of the altar. Next, Hanna and I, her arm hooked in mine, proceeded up the aisle. She was wearing a beautiful wedding dress made by her godmother, and carried a bridle bouquet of red roses. I wore my dress blue Navy uniform with the red 2nd class petty officer chevrons on my upper sleeve. We walked up the aisle to the altar in rhythm to the wedding music being played on an old, majestic organ. I was quite nervous, as was Hanna.

The German pastor went through the marriage ceremony in German with a bunch of church text I wasn't that familiar with. I slipped the ring on and we were pronounced man and wife. The old church bells chimed and the people went out of the church and stood around the front waiting for the bride and groom. When we stepped out they congratulated us and pictures were taken.

The reception was right after the wedding ceremony in Hanna's parents' apartment. The sliding doors between the living room and a large bedroom next to it were opened up to make one large reception area, and the bedroom furniture was moved out. Tables and chairs were set for about 35 or so people, mostly relatives and friends.

Things started off a little slow at the reception because no one took charge of serving drinks right away, but after a while people were helping themselves and feeling good. The meal was cooked by a neighbor across the street, which the guests enjoyed. I had the wedding cake baked by a German baker, who worked in the PX. He wasn't aware of the multilevel wedding cakes made in the United States that I had wanted. What we got was a single-layer cake with a round top, fancy decorations, and a trellis with a bride and groom statue.

After marriage service in church, coming out with two flower children

Alte Kirche (old church) we were married in, built in the 1500s

Wedding party in front of church

My mother, who flew in from Chicago, and Hanna's mother

After the cake was cut and served, the music started and people danced in the hallway. Afterward, Hanna threw a small wedding bouquet over her shoulder to the young, unmarried women, and then the women ripped Hanna's veil apart and took pieces for good luck.

Everybody ended up having a good time and the festivities lasted until the middle of the night, the pastor and my mother right along with everyone else.

My mother, by coincidence, had lived in Bremerhaven for some years before she immigrated to the U.S., and had friends there. She had planned to attend my wedding, go see her Bremerhaven friends beforehand, and then travel southward by train to the Frankfurt area in central Germany. She planned to go to a small town near Frankfurt where she was born and raised as a child, stay with some old friends a few days, and then fly back from Frankfurt to the U.S.

Well, it so happened that Hanna and I were going to Herrenalb in the Black Forest for our honeymoon, an hour or two farther south than where my mother was going. We would be driving south on the autobahn from Bremerhaven and would pass the area where she wanted to go. Our plans also were to leave early the morning after the wedding.

So, I told my mother she could ride with us and we would drop her off in Schneidhain, her place of birth. I figured it wouldn't take more than seven or eight hours to get there, so if we left early enough we could be there later in the afternoon while it was still light.

We didn't get up early enough the next morning and we left late. The weather wasn't good. It rained off and on, which slowed the traffic down. Then, while driving at high speeds to keep up with fast drivers on the autobahn, our car started to rumble, bump up and down, and pull to one side. Sure enough, we had a flat tire on our rented German Ford. I pulled over on the side of the autobahn as much as I could, but it still looked like a dangerous situation for changing a tire with the heavy traffic and racecar drivers.

The autobahn had service vehicles that cruised around and watched for car problems. No cell phones at that time. So, we waited an hour until a service car spotted us. We got the tire changed, but we were now a couple of hours behind schedule. As we drove southward the traffic moved slower and slower in the rush hour.

It started to get dark and we were still some distance from where we would drop my mother off. Suddenly, it was getting really dark with cloud cover from the rain and dusk. I started to worry about how I would find my way from the turnoff from the autobahn, through the miles of unknown side streets to Schneidhain in the dark—and then get back on the autobahn and find our way into the hills in the Black Forest. No way, I decided.

The windshield wipers whipped back and forth and became a little nerve-racking. "Lets stop at a rest house along the autobahn and stay overnight," I said nervously. Hanna and my mother agreed.

We stopped at the next rest house. "We would like two rooms for one night."

"Unschulding sie mich, wir haben kein Zimmer frei." (Sorry, we have no rooms free.) We got back in the car and stopped at the next place we came to. Same thing, "...kein Zimmer frei." They were filled up, too. We started to worry that we might get stranded and end up sleeping in the car. The third rest house had only one room available with a king-size bed.

My mother said, "Let's not go any farther. Let's take the room. You two can sleep in the bed and I'll sleep on a chair in the lobby."

Hanna and I looked at each other and said we couldn't do that, but maybe we could all sleep in the king-size bed. Did they have fold-away beds? "Nein." It was thus decided we would take the room with the one big bed—and that's how it came to pass that Hanna and I slept with my mother in the same bed on the first day of our honeymoon!

Well, we made it through the night because we were tired. I like to joke that my mother slept between us, but that's not true. The next day we woke up refreshed, had a nice breakfast and traveled on to my mother's hometown of Schneidhain. It was difficult, but we found the tiny little town even though it was off the beaten track.

My mother's friends were joyous in seeing us and talked Hanna and me into staying there all day and into attending a big celebration the town was having that night, with an oompa band, dancing, sauerkraut, potato salad, bratwurst, and lots of beer. We stayed and a neighbor let Hanna and I sleep in a very beautiful guest bedroom they had. The next morning we woke up with a bright sun shining through the white lace curtains. We had a wonderful breakfast and they served us graciously. We then packed up, thanked them, said goodbye to my mother, and wished her fun on the rest of her trip and a good flight home.

My wife and I went onward the next morning, leaving my mother there, drove back to the autobahn, and farther south into the Black Forest. When we got to Heidelberg we did some sightseeing there during the day and ended up staying overnight, even though we had lost almost a couple of days already. We viewed the Nectar River, the Old Town area, and the old castle with the gigantic wine barrels.

The next morning it was on the road again, but we were getting closer to our destination. We drove the curves and ups and downs of the beautiful, low, green foothill mountains of the Black Forest and finally arrived at our destination of Herrenalb.

It was a small resort and health spa-type town nestled alongside a low Alpine Mountain. We stayed at a three-story pension home. Much to our surprise, we found out when we got back to the U.S. that it was the same pension house that one of Hanna's best German friends, Hilde, had worked at as an apprentice when she was young before she immigrated to the U.S.

Honeymoon in the Black Forest

We felt great to be there. The sun was shining, they fed us at the pension home, and we relaxed. In the afternoon we strolled through beautiful park and forest areas and ate fresh strawberry shortcake with whipping cream. It was one of the happiest days in both our lives. The next day we went swimming in a big pool that was filled with chilly mountain stream water. That evening after a super meal we watched a movie in the public park put on for the public, *The Inspector General* with Danny Kaye. The German language was dubbed in, which sounded very strange to me.

But all this good stuff didn't last very long. The jinx was still on us. The following day, day number four, Hanna woke up with a terrible toothache. Aspirin and other remedies didn't work. At the end of the afternoon it was obvious things were not going to get better, so we asked our landlord if there were any dentists around. He recommended one in a neighboring town, Heilbronn. We made an emergency appointment and went there the next morning. We also called my mother in Schneidhain and she said she would come there by train and help us.

The German dentist examined the tooth. I don't think he took any x-rays, but said it was a bad abscess, the tooth couldn't be saved, and he yanked it out. However, Hanna wasn't much relieved on this, the fifth day of our honeymoon. She was in pain the rest of the day and much of the next day. My mother helped nurse her and then went back to her hometown via the train again. So much for those two days of our honeymoon.

After the tooth problem got better, we did some further sightseeing in the Black Forest around Herrenalb, and places such as Baden-Baden, the capital of Germany for some years and a town with a swanky casino. A little bewildered and disappointed with the hang-ups on our honeymoon, we then returned to Bremerhaven and on to London the next day. It was now late in June.

Before I left London for my wedding in Germany, I moved out of the room I shared with another guy that I worked with, and moved into a larger flat with a kitchen facility, in a large, frame boarding house in the Hempstead Heath area of London. We moved in there when we went back after the wedding.

I took a double-decker bus to work; I think it was the 59A. I sat on the topside right in front and enjoyed the scenery as the bus drove down Regent Street along Regent Park, and down the famous Sherlock Holmes' Baker Street to Oxford Street. I got off there and walked a short way to Grosvenor's Square.

After we were in our apartment in Hempstead Heath a couple of months, Hanna had problems with her feet and we had to buy special support shoes for her. In the meantime, we became aware that she was pregnant with our first daughter, Bernice. This came up unexpectedly to us both. Other complications popped up, such as swollen legs and morning sickness. It also frightened us, because of our ignorance of pregnancy care, and because we were sort of all alone in London, away from help from our parents and friends.

The apartment we rented in Hempstead Heath
in London after we were married

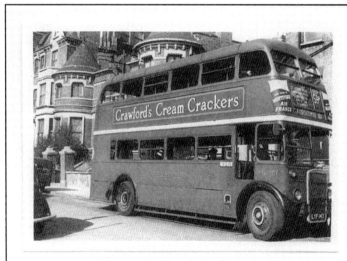

*Herb took double decker bus from West Hemstead
to Grovensnor Square, where he worked.
The house we lived in is right behind the bus.*

I road a red, double-decker bus to work in Grosvenor Square.

Chapter 16

ELUSIVE VISA;
ZIGZAG ROUTE TO U.S.

I encountered another big, red tape entanglement in getting a visa for Hanna to come to the United States. Even though Hanna, a German citizen, was married to an American citizen, it did not automatically give her the right to enter the U.S. We had to get a visa for her, involving American and German background information and documents. If they found something negative about Hanna or her family, it could well be they wouldn't grant the visa.

I checked in June when I got back to London on the status of the visa. "Don't know." I checked in July. "Nothing." Come August and September they still didn't know what the status was or they didn't want to go through the bother of checking. I told them I was being discharged in October and I needed the visa by then. We became worried that there was some hang-up in granting the visa.

On it went. In October, when it was obvious the visa process would not be finished, I made provisions for when I had to leave for New York for the discharge, and for Hanna to stay with a married sailor I worked with, a savvy guy, until the visa came through. His wife was American and they had a fairly large apartment in London. I asked him if he could help me out. At first he was reluctant, but I told him I would pay for all of Hanna's living expenses, and rent also—a generous amount. I explained that Hanna was an honest, decent, quiet person who both he and his wife would have no problems getting along with. I told him I chose him because he was a regular in the Navy and was experienced with the Navy personnel office and the American embassy.

Before I left, I made a tentative reservation for Hanna for the flight to Washington, D.C. on a Military Air Transport System plane, and hoped it would work. The MATS flights were for military personnel and their families. Also, transportation from London to the Air Force base where the American Air Force was stationed would also have to be made once the visa came in.

My co-worker friend recognized the difficulties involved and knew the ins and outs of the rules and red tape system. He agreed, even though it was an imposition for him, but I had to push him for some help. The whole process was too detailed and tricky for a German-speaking person to get through alone in London.

I was able to fly back to New York instead of taking the MSTS as I had when I came, a couple of weeks before my actual discharge. I was back in the Brooklyn Navy Yard again sitting around, pulling some duty here or there, otherwise I could go out to Manhattan.

The plan was that Hanna would send a telegram to me at the Brooklyn Navy Yard confirming her flight arrival time, which was at Dulles International Airport. If there were delays or changes from what arrangements I made before I left, she would let me know. The telegram came a few days before she left. She was scheduled to arrive in the middle of the night about 1:30 a.m.

Ironically, on the day she was to arrive in D.C., I was assigned duty at the Brooklyn Navy Yard that evening. I explained to the officer of the day the problem I had and asked to be released from the duty. He didn't think too much of the idea and wasn't too anxious to go through the hassle of changing it. I further explained that my wife could hardly speak English and knew nothing about the U.S. and Washington, that she was arriving in the middle of the night, and that I had reservations at a hotel there. Also, I had plane tickets for both my wife and I to get to New York, where I would finish my discharge procedure. Finally, he said "All right, all right! I'll get you off of duty." And he did.

I flew from New York to Dulles during the day, checked into the hotel room, ate a late dinner and went to Dulles to wait for a few hours for the plane to arrive. It finally arrived, a couple of hours late, at 3:30 a.m. Hanna looked exasperated and disheveled coming out of customs. We hugged and were happy and relieved that we were together again. We got the luggage and took a taxi to the hotel in D.C. After a fairly good night of sleep we ate breakfast, went to the Dulles Airport and flew to New York. In New York, we hopped in a taxi again, and checked in at a hotel in Manhattan.

"We went from one place to another, up and down, landings and takeoffs." Hanna related that it was an unbelievably horrible flight. She had left London nearly three days ago. Instead of a nonstop overseas flight from London to New York, as you might do today, the MATS flight was more like a shuttle bus going east and west and north and south. The flight picked up military people from all over the place and had a limited flying range. The first leg was from London to Portugal. The second leg went on to Morocco in Northern Africa, where they had to stay overnight. More military personnel and family members got on and off at each point.

There wasn't much pressurization control on the plane, if any. Canvas seats lined each side of the plane and they were uncomfortable. The third leg took off from Morocco the next day and flew to the Azores in the middle of the Atlantic. You might think the fourth leg would go straight away to D.C. No such luck. It flew way farther north to the northeast corner of Canada, Newfoundland, where they overnighted again. Then, they finally did the fifth and last leg of the zigzaggy journey, and flew off from Newfoundland late in the afternoon, arriving in the middle of the night in D.C.

Hanna sat next to an English woman on the plane who was a great help. She was married to an American and was able to handle the language for Hanna. Without her as a companion, Hanna felt she never would have survived the flight.

Back at the Brooklyn Navy Yard, my official honorable discharge papers were completed a few days early and we were able to fly to our final destination of Chicago. We were happy we got through the whole ordeal of the red tape with the marriage, episodes on the honeymoon, a nail-biter with getting the visa, and leaving Hanna alone in London, then the misery of the military flight.

Flashing back to a few months before my discharge, while in London, there was an important factor I haven't mentioned yet. I was notified I was eligible to take the 1st class petty officer test in August, 1955. If I passed it, I would advance from the 2nd class petty officer rating I currently had to 1st class petty officer. I studied diligently and felt I did well on the tests. But the results on how you did on the test and the official advancement wouldn't come until a couple of months after my discharge.

When I was home and a civilian again they notified me I had passed and had a 3.6 score, one of the highest scores in the Navy. I presume the 3.6 meant out of a possible 4.0. Had I known that I would be a 1st class petty officer within four years, a rate where things get nicer for you in the Navy, I might have stayed in a little longer.

Part IV

BACK ON AMERICAN SOIL

Chapter 17
LIFE IN THE U.S. AGAIN

Family, Children, Jobs, Education

My parents were waiting at the O'Hare Airport in Chicago when we arrived from the Naval station in New York in October 1955. We all hugged and were happy to see each other again. It had been almost two years that I was gone. My mother had told us that we could stay at their house in Chicago for the first few months until we were settled. I had to get a civilian job, buy a car, and Hanna and I then had to look for an apartment to live in and prepare for our first child.

At this time Hanna was pregnant about four months. Somehow, since she had seen a doctor about her pregnancy in London in August, and things were okay, we didn't give going to a doctor again much thought. But her legs were starting to swell up and a couple of months later, as we got closer to the delivery date, we went to a doctor in Chicago. How ignorant and careless we were.

He examined her, and to our horror, he found she had toxemia. He told us both the baby and mother could potentially die if it was not taken care of right away. We couldn't wait. He added, "Hanna, you have to go into the hospital and have the baby induced as soon as possible, even though it's a month too early—or risk the welfare of your baby and maybe your own life."

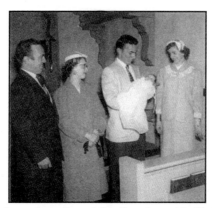

The baptism of our first child, Bernice, with Godparents,
my brother Paul and sister-in-law Annegret, at Luther
Memorial Church on Wilson and Campbell in 1956

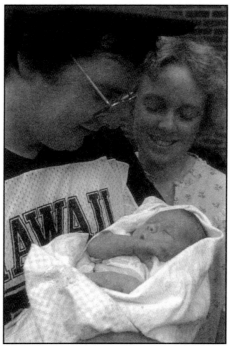

Our first grandchild, Jeffery, with parents,
Peter and Bernice, in 1982

We checked into Ravenswood Hospital on the north side of Chicago and they hooked Hanna up for the inducement. Nothing happened for a couple of days, so they tried something stronger. On the third day, February 21, 1956 our first daughter Bernice was born four weeks ahead of time. Hanna was okay and Bernice was healthy and normal; a joyous occasion. Hanna stayed in the hospital for four or five days for observation and as a precaution. Then I took her back to my mother's house where we had been staying. Bernice was a beautiful baby with a magical baby smile and a pleasant, thoughtful personality. We were indeed lucky. After some weeks we found our first of two apartments we lived in in Chicago, left my mother's house, and moved in.

It was a small basement apartment in a two-story brick building on Patterson Avenue near Addison and Lincoln Avenue in Chicago. The rent was $45 a month. The only bedroom was barely big enough to get a queen-size bed and a dresser in it. If you slept on the wall side you had to crawl across the bed to get in and out. The front room was just barely big enough for a sofa, one easy chair, end and coffee tables, a TV, and we squeezed Bernice's baby crib in, too. The kitchen was an average size and the back door led into the basement, where there was a laundry area for the tenants to do their washing.

My first job upon returning was as a draftsman for $1.50 an hour at the General Blower Company in Morton Grove, a suburb northwest of Chicago, which manufactured industrial fans. It was a typical musty, oily environment with loud metal working equipment in the shop banging away all day. The head of the drafting department, a tall, sloppy, heavyset guy usually with a toothpick in the side of his mouth, spent a lot of time chasing a short married woman who worked in the office. The engineer in charge of design and testing fans was a chain smoker and a nervous wreck.

There was another draftsman, a six-and-a-half-foot-tall monster of a guy, a little bit like a half punch drunk boxer, who was afraid that I was going to get ahead of him in the drafting department. He made indirect comments that I might get thrown into Lake Michigan with concrete shoes if I didn't watch out.

The drafting I had to do was elementary and boring, so after a few months, and because of the characters I worked with, I decided this was not the place for a career. I searched around and found a want ad in the *Chicago Tribune* for a draftsmen at a sheet metal air conditioning company in Chicago. The pay was a half a buck more than the previous job—$2.00 an hour. I applied and got the job, thus the beginning of my career in heating and air conditioning at the Mellish and Murray Company.

My intentions were to work during the day at a mechanical engineering related job, and go to school and study mechanical engineering in college at night on the G.I. bill, which would cover the tuition.

I started my college education in February of 1956, four months after we got back from Germany. I enrolled in two evening classes at Wright Junior College on the northwest side of Chicago. I took college algebra and an economics class. I also took a general education test (GED) and was able to get 24 college credit hours without taking some 100 college classes such as English, math, and other courses, which counted toward my engineering credits. So, after I passed the first two courses with good grades, I already had about 30 credit hours toward my degree after one semester, equivalent to about one year of schooling. I went a second semester to Wright Jr. taking algebra and a general psychology class.

I did well, and then decided to transfer to a four-year engineering program at the Illinois Institute of Technology, IIT, a few miles south of downtown Chicago. I attended there for over eight years at night, while working full-time.

Some of the engineering professors had no mercy. Over holidays like Thanksgiving and Christmas they gave you twice as many homework problems to solve than otherwise. One professor in one of my mechanical engineering classes assigned us eight difficult problems to work through, including "calculate mathematically using calculus and with heat transfer formulas how long does it take to cook a 20-pound turkey?" He gave us a hint on how to start—"Assume the turkey is the shape of a football." That killed my Thanksgiving holiday.

After I completed over eight years of going to school in the evenings, I applied to take the State of Illinois Engineering Certification test. The two-day test was comprehensive and it covered the academics of a bachelor's degree in engineering, plus the subsequent four years of actual experience. You also had to solve problems in eight engineering disciplines, as well as in your own specialized field.

I was worried about passing such a long and difficult examination. Then I heard that the state of Illinois offered an eight-week review course of sample problems and solutions on the test, which was taught by outstanding professors from the University of Illinois. I took the eight-week course, a marvelous summary of the engineering disciplines. It helped me to pass the certification test without much trouble, even though half of the engineers taking the test fail at it. I became a certified engineer in Illinois, could certify engineering designs, and could open up my own consulting engineering firm, if I so desired.

After a couple of years in the basement apartment we moved into a ground floor apartment on Hoyne Avenue in Chicago, because we wanted two bedrooms. However, the bedrooms were tiny—hardly big enough to squeeze a bed in them. We slept in one of them, which had a bed and a small night table crammed in it, and Bernice slept in the other bedroom in a bunk bed underneath a sloping staircase. You had to duck under the staircase or you would bump your head on it. Things really weren't much better than the basement apartment except the living room and kitchen were bigger. The washing machine was in the bathroom. I had to carry oil in a five-gallon can from the garage outside for the oil heater in the center of the apartment, which did a crumby job of heating. But for $40 a month rent, who could complain?

Then in 1959, just before our second child was born, my wife and

I decided to buy a house in the suburbs and not fight the inconvenience of small, old apartments in Chicago. We searched the north and west areas of Chicago for a suitable house at a price we could afford, within a reasonable driving distance from where I worked. After searching relentlessly and being almost ready to give up, we stumbled on a town, Elk Grove Village, located 25 miles northwest of Chicago.

We found a house in a modern suburban development built by Centex, a Texas homebuilder. They started building the Elk Grove Village complex in 1957 and sold a record number of houses, built at breakneck speeds, for many years. It mushroomed up into a gigantic suburb from its original farmland beginnings, and was surrounded by a forest, O'Hare Airport, an expressway (which came later), and more farmland. There was one store in town when we moved there, but the schools, libraries, police and fire stations didn't sprout up until Elk Grove Village grew and grew.

I asked myself, *What am I getting into?* My answer was a 30-year mortgage which I could barely pay each month, a loan of $3,500 that I borrowed from my father for the down payment at six percent interest, and immensely increased time and transportation costs to work and back. The house itself was a bargain package. This efficient builder gave you a *beat the market price* for a ranch house with three bedrooms, closet space, a modern bathroom, a dining area, a living room with a picture window, an attached garage which kept your car warm in the cold Chicago winters, and a nice sized lot with a patio area. It seemed like a dream at the time, all for $17,500.

However, after I was in the new suburban house for a couple of years the reality of the circumstances whacked me on the side of the head. I inherited a strenuously crammed and busy schedule. It was a long way from my job and school. I got up at 6:00 a.m. and drove a total of over three hours every day, mostly in rush hour traffic, early in the morning to work near downtown Chicago. Then, after working a full day, I drove a distance to IIT on the south side for engineering classes at night.

160

Finally, bleary eyed, I ended up getting home about 10:30 or 11 o'clock at night. There were always some problems awaiting me, which my wife brought up when I got home. There was a sock stuck in the drain from the dryer, or one of the kids was jumping on the bed, fell, hit the corner of the bed board and poked a hole in the top of her nose. Plus there was no respite on weekends. I spent most of the time doing homework, gardening, and house projects, and since we had only one car then, I had to take my wife shopping.

So, I was busy all the time at work, at school, and at home. Hanna took care of most other things, the children, meals, housework, and more.

And to add to that, during this nine-year period from 1956 to 1965, while I was being educated at IIT, advancing at work, and moving into a new house—the family grew. We were blessed with three more healthy, beautiful children after Bernice was born—Mike, Tarna, and Jamie. Every child had their own personality and nice features. My wife dressed them beautifully and got them to school and church on time. We were happy with our growing family and status in the world.

Our First Child, Bernice

Continuing on with my oldest daughter, Bernice, who is a baby boomer.... She is intelligent, disciplined, responsible, rational, kind, understanding, tolerant, and a *do it right the first time*-type person, like her mother. She went to Northern University in Illinois and became a registered nurse. She was an excellent, studious student. She graduated summa cum laude, which means *a very high grade average, with the highest praise.* And she did it in 3 ½ years instead of four. In high school she excelled in advanced mathematics, college calculus, and other areas.

Patterson Ave.
Chicago 1957

Our first daughter Bernice with my wife and her sister,
in front of our basement apartment

We paid half of her school costs and she paid the other half. No student loans. We had a policy with our kids that they could spend half the money they got for birthdays, Christmas, and so on, and the other half would be saved for their schooling. So, she had a chunk of money at the start of college, and earned the balance working summers and part-time at school for the first two or three years. We kept this policy up for all four kids and they were self-disciplined enough to make it work.

After Bernice graduated from college as a registered nurse, she got married to Peter in 1978 and went on to have three boys; Jeffery, the oldest; Ryan, the middle; and Michael, the youngest.

Jeffrey graduated as a business major from Illinois State University, got married, and had two children. In recent years he got divorced and now lives temporarily with his parents, Bernice and Peter.

Ryan went to Illinois State also, for about one and a half years, then moved back home and lived with his parents for some years. He now lives elsewhere and is working in a doctor's office.

Michael Robertson just graduated from the University of Illinois in Champaign as a software engineer, with high grades, and received several job offers. He took a job with IBM in Austin, Texas.

Our Second Child, Michael

Michael Wendes was born four years after Bernice, on November 4, 1959 also at Ravenswood Hospital. He weighed 7.1 pounds at birth and became quite chubby as a toddler.

Michael grew up in Elk Grove Village. We lived by a forest preserve and he romped through the forest like Tom Sawyer or Abraham Lincoln and was familiar with the whole tract of land. After graduating from high school he went to Southern Illinois University near St. Louis to study photography, and graduated with a graphics art degree. He produced some fine pictures in school.

He worked at a couple of jobs the first few years out of college, photographing foods for Quaker Oats, Kraft Foods, and others. As a freelance photographer he found projects on a contract basis didn't last forever and were hard to come by. There were gaps in between the contracts, so he formed his own commercial photographic company taking photos of industrial machinery for catalogues. That was tougher yet, especially when working mostly alone setting up lights, scaffolding, cameras, electrical connections, and synchronizing the whole photographic process. After eight years, some quite successful, others not so busy, he decided to get out of the difficulties of the business, running around as a one-man professional photographic company doing everything, including sales and getting jobs. Maybe with a partner, which the business really required, things could have turned out better.

There were mitigating personal life circumstances for Michael, which occurred during his first decade out of school and working at the various photographic jobs. He married his first wife, but things didn't go well and after five years, they ended up getting divorced.

For a few years after that he had a couple more relationships, but they were not really the right ones.

It was about this time that he felt a little disappointed with how things were going. We told him he could move in with us until he readjusted to his divorce and made some changes in his career. He lived with us for a year and a half. He tried a couple of jobs, one at selling for a printing company and another at a commercial mailing service. Neither were the best long range ways to go.

So we then decided to thoroughly review, with him, his capabilities, knowledge, education and personality; determine what was a good job market for his talents and knowledge and what would be the best possible shift in his career. At first he had some inkling of becoming a truck driver. My wife and I felt strongly that the best area for jobs and growth was somewhere in the computer industry and that he was better suited in that area. He ended up agreeing and he formulated a plan and schedule of taking Microsoft service courses in Computer Information Systems and completed an online curriculum at a university in Phoenix.

He became certified in most Microsoft service areas, and has a Master's of Science in Computer Information Systems.

He was able to start at a training position, and it took off from there. He continually sought other jobs to expand his career in recent years. He worked with the imaging division of the Japanese Canon Corporation for some years. He was an electronic troubleshooter at O'Hare Airport in Chicago, not only being responsible for keeping the computer systems of the airlines working, but also their many other electronic devices. He also has worked in a Computer Technical Support position with a high school in the northwest suburbs of Chicago, helping to keep teachers, staff, and students operating on their computers.

Several years ago Mike met a professional woman, Carol, and he married her. She has three daughters by a previous marriage.

Our four children with spouses. Left to right:
First couple, Bernice and Peter...Second couple, Tarna and Dave...
Third couple, Jamie and Ismael...Fourth person, my wife's sister
Annegret...Right-end couple, Mike and Carol

My wife and I with grandchildren and great-grandchildren

Our Third Child, Tarna

My wife and I made up the name for our third child, Tarna. We didn't know if it would be a boy or a girl so we decided if it was a boy, we would name him Todd. But if it was a girl we thought... hmmm...we could just change the boy's name from Todd to a girl's name, Tarna, and so we did. She was born on March 14, 1962, again at the same hospital where our first two children were born, Ravenswood.

Her full name at birth was *Tarna Luise Wendes* (the middle name after her grandmother in Germany on her mother's side).

Tarna was a bubbly and affectionate child. She attended Elk Grove grammar schools and high school, and then went to Northern University in DeKalb, Illinois, graduating in specialized education, teaching children with problems. She taught a problem fifth grade class a year or two in Waukegan, Illinois. She did well, but decided to devote herself to being a wife and mother raising her four children.

She married David Eskoff, who she met at Northern University in July, 1985, the year after she graduated. Dave graduated with a master's degree in business and accounting.

Tarna and Dave have four nice, intelligent children. She is a loving, no-nonsense mother, an excellent home manager and popular social director. The first born was Cory Eskoff, on March 6th, 1987. His elementary and high schooling was mostly in Crystal Lake, IL and he graduated as a business major from Illinois State University in 2009. He is currently living and working in Chicago and is not married.

The second child that Tarna had was also a boy, Cameron Eskoff, born April 3rd, 1990. He also grew up and attended primary schools and high school in Crystal Lake. Cameron must have some genes from a tall basketball player in his ancestry, because he shot up to about six-foot-two or so and towers over the rest of the people in our family. He is a pleasant, thoughtful person. He is currently studying for a master's degree in business and accounting at

Northern Illinois University and will take his certified public accounting test at graduation, also. He is currently engaged to be married.

Tarna and Dave's third child is Megan Eskoff, born on August 8th, 1993. A five-pound baby, she was brought home from the hospital, gained weight and everything was all right. She has attractive brown eyes and dark hair and a bright smile. Like her siblings, she went to Crystal Lake schools, and excelled in most subjects. She wants to become a writer, has shown talent in this direction, and has completed two years of college to date. She got a scholarship at the Art Institute in Chicago in creative writing and is attending there for her degree in fine arts, for the last two years.

The fourth and last child born to Tarna and Dave is Chloe Eskoff, on June 20th, 1997 in Crystal Lake. Like her older two brothers and sister, she's an intelligent, good student and will be finishing high school in two years. Also, like her older sister she has an attractive smile and brown eyes, brown hair.

That covers the Eskoff family to date, and they are going along very fine as a family.

Our Fourth Child, Jamie

Our fourth and last child was born Jamie Rose Wendes on January 27, 1964. She is now Jamie DeLaCruz, by her second marriage. She grew up in Elk Grove and attended Elk Grove elementary, middle, and high schools there, in this neat and modern suburban village.

She was a sweet, cute, and calm child with an unassuming and peaceful nature, who walked and ate by herself in her baby years earlier than her siblings. She has grown to be a pleasant, non-aggressive person. She is artistically talented and attended Northern Illinois University for five years and graduated with a bachelor's degree in graphic arts in 1987. While attending her years of master's studies, she had a graduate assistant position teaching.

Tarna and Jamie in their McDonald's
uniforms working after school

While working at her first job at Moore Business Forms in the north suburbs of Chicago, she bought a condo in a northwest suburb of Chicago. After a few years she met her first husband, Ralph David Herzog. They became engaged and married in March of 1993. They had three children; Maxwell in January 1994, a pleasant, unassuming personality; Mary was born in July of 1996, an attractive, serious and nice girl; and Caleb's birth was in January 2000. He has unique instincts and intuitiveness, is unusually observant, and comes up with surprising adult questions about things.

Problems occurred in the marriage and she and Ralph got a divorce. Jamie went on for the next few years with her three children. Then Jamie met her second husband, Ismael DeLaCruz, who is from

Mexico, at the church she went to. He was educated as a veterinarian in Mexico. He had been in the U.S. for a number of years and has two attractive, talented, well-behaved teenaged children with beautiful black hair, from his previous marriage; a girl, Marcela, who displays artistic talents; and a boy, Sebastian, who has musical talent and was very active in music in high school.

Romance took its course and Jamie and Ismael got married in 2010. Before then Jamie lived in the second-floor apartment of a two-story house in Crystal Lake, IL. Then suddenly the first floor apartment became available. The combined size of the two apartments was more than enough comfortable living space for Jamie and Ismael, and their five children.

All has been working out fairly well for them. Jamie has built up a small home sewing business for herself, which she is very proficient at. She also works part-time at her church. Ismael is building up a landscaping company with a partner. The two oldest boys recently have just graduated from high school and are working and deciding on what careers they want and where they want to go to college.

I have been blessed with my education, a successful career, safe and comfortable homes to live in, and a loving wife, children and grandchildren. Although it was always busy and somewhat stressful, I thoroughly enjoyed this phase of my life.

Chapter 18

BUSY CAREER AS ENGINEER

My family grew and grew—one, two, three, four children over a period of eight years. When the second child was born in 1959 we moved from our old small apartment in Chicago into a new house in the blossoming suburbs. The fourth child was born in January of 1964 during my eighth year of attending college in the evenings. At the same time my experience, skills, knowledge, and confidence expanded. The sour image and mischievous behavior was behind me and a serious and motivated attitude took its place as I plowed on, shooting for success.

My engineering career actually started in 1955 when I returned to the U.S. from service in Europe. I worked a few months at my first job in the musty conditions at the fan company as an engineering draftsman. The opportunity to get out of that job came when I saw an ad in the *Chicago Tribune* for an HVAC draftsman. I called them for an interview and went there with neat sample drawings, and a short resume: "Top grades in high school drafting classes, four years of technical work in the Navy, and three months of drawing fans for General Blower."

They hired me right off. I quit my old job and I started to work for them shortly thereafter. It was the Mellish and Murray Company, a heating, ventilation, and air conditioning (HVAC) construction contractor.

The shop was in Chicago, two miles west of the downtown area in an old, shabby neighborhood near Ashland and Lake Street. The neighborhood was being converted to an industrial area with the remnants of the old residential buildings slowly disappearing. A couple blocks south of where the Mellish and Murray plant was located, bordering Lake Street, were the Chicago Housing Authority high rise apartment buildings.

Little did I know that when I started there, not only would I be working for the 80-year-old grandfather who started the company in the late 1800s, but also his son, who was in his 50s, and two rather outspoken grandchildren, fighting-type Irishmen sons about my age.

I was with them for over 20 years, starting in 1956 and leaving them in1977. The grandfather retired a few years after I started. He mainly came in to sign checks while he was there. The son, Harold, ran the company, and died at an early age of 54 due to a gall bladder problem. Thereafter, the two rambunctious Murray brothers, who started just before I did, ruled the company. The older brother, Jim, became the president; and Charles, the younger one, the financial officer. There was also a sister who worked there for a while, and then moved to Colorado with her husband.

I fit into the organization because I was a low-key engineering-type guy, while they were outgoing managers whose egos and status sort of guided them. Jim was like a fighting Irishman during those years. He sort of relished jumping into the constant conflicts between other contractors, architects, engineers, and owners over scheduling, responsibility for items in or not covered by the plans and specs, timely payments, and getting paid for extras.

After starting as a draftsmen, during my 22 years there I rose up the ranks to estimator, project manager, designer, and head of the engineering department. Finally, I became vice president of the construction division.

After some years of being with Mellish I also became an instructor and taught union HVAC mechanics and office personnel in an evening school. It was financed by a union schooling program and the contractor's association.

I taught four different courses related to the actual work I was performing at the Mellish and Murray Company. The first course was on estimating HVAC jobs, the second on testing and balancing HVAC systems, the third on Energy Savings, and the fourth on

171

managing HVAC companies for profit. Also concurrently, I wrote HVAC articles on the topics, which were published in *Heating, Piping and Air Conditioning* and *SNIPS* magazines.

Industry Plagued with Archaic Estimating System

In the beginning years at Mellish and Murray I sat in the engineering room at a drawing board drafting, another draftsman sat at his board, and an estimator sat at a desk. I listened to the estimator and the owner of the contracting company putting the final figures together on bids for HVAC construction projects as I was doing my drafting. This was my entry into the estimating mess they had at that time.

The boss said, "It looks like the cost of the galvanized ductwork should be $61,000."

The estimator responded, "I really think it is a cheaper ductwork job, and it should be $58,000, but I'll go along with whatever you say, boss."

The owner, now not sure of his judgment, and worried that his "guesstimate" price might not be right and too high for the market, said, "Let's ask the field superintendent what he thinks."

The superintendent was called into the office. He wasn't familiar with the blueprints at all at this point, but looked at them briefly to get a gut feeling about the value of the ductwork. "It looks like an average ductwork job to me, $63,000."

Then the boss made a decision. "Okay, thank you for your input, but let's go with $60,000. I think that's best."

Everybody obediently nodded their heads that that was okay with them. They submitted the bid and were overjoyed that they were low and would get the contract on the job. After the project was completed, the boss looked at their cost accounting figures from the bookkeeper on the ductwork. Cost figures on jobs came back to the boss secretly, only to him, and were not broadcasted to the employees. He believed that only the owner should be privy to such information.

He gasped when he saw that the ductwork costs turned out to be almost 20 percent higher than the $60,000 put in the bid. It was a loss of $12,000 on the ductwork portion of the project.

The owner didn't let anybody know, not even the estimator, about the loss, but he complained that the shop and field mechanics must have been sleeping on the job, and chided the estimator for not knowing the correct cost figures better. He felt that his estimating figure of $60,000 was really correct and didn't do any further analysis as to what really happened.

Ugh, I thought. *There has got to be a better way.* I checked around with other HVAC contractors in Chicago. Sure enough, they all estimated the ductwork the same way, with an inaccurate, outdated method. I swore to myself, if I ever got to be an estimator I would come up with a better ductwork cost estimating system. So, I began to work on it.

Revolutionizing the Faulty System

I became the assistant to the estimator after a few years of drafting and helped the estimator with various parts of the bids. After some years, HVAC systems became more sophisticated in the United States, and the estimator at our contracting company made more and more mistakes. He had trouble handling the technical changes in the industry. I kept doing more estimating work, trying out different methods, and letting the president of our company know what my ideas and findings were. I came up with better, more accurate figures on estimates. It took years, lots of research, and lots of time studying.

I analyzed the problems in pricing ductwork systems, and found out they were based on invalid assumptions and not breaking down the factors enough that went into the cost of ductwork. The risk in bidding projects was that the actual costs figures could vary (would you believe up to 50 percent higher or lower than the average typical job?) without the estimator being aware of it at the time of bidding— not just plus or minus 20 percent, as in my example. This happens mainly because of lumping all the ductwork cost factors together, which impinge on the costs. Ductwork systems were all tossed in the same meat grinder in the estimating process and would end up as an indistinguishable batch of ground beef, cost-wise.

This ineptitude in estimating ductwork by many contractors was caused by tradition, habit, and ignorance. The lump-sum estimating had been passed down from generation to generation and accepted as an industry practice and norm.

Improved Ductwork Cost Estimating

Some goals and objectives had to be determined to start off with, to reach a more accurate system of estimating ductwork. Optional new methods of estimating had to be developed and tested out, cost records expanded. I conducted this research and testing, and came up with a system that reduced the plus or minus accuracy to four or five percent. Even with this more sophisticated method of estimating ductwork costs, it was not the final answer to acceptable estimating accuracy in the HVAC industry. Computers and software would be needed to make it more accurate yet, and they had to reach some maturity in order to write the extensive software needed for estimating the ductwork costs very accurately.

This needed development occurred in the 1970s, '80s and '90s. Most of my development of the new method of estimating was performed at Mellish and Murray Company, before I resigned my position in 1977. I opened up my own consultant engineering firm. I did some consulting and conducted seminars, but slowly went into being a full-time software developer. I was able to develop a very accurate, realistic, user-friendly cost estimating software program because of my extensive background in the industry during these years.

I hired some programmers who came and went. Then, finally, two skillful, talented programmers stayed on, Jim and my nephew Tim. They became the experts in the estimating programs for sheet metal and piping. They are still with the company today, but working for Joe, who bought my company from me. These two major software programs are still being sold today.

Cadillac in front of my consulting engineer office in Elk Grove Village

Finally, we ended up with two comprehensive, complete, user-friendly major estimating programs. It had built into it formulas and comprehensive labor hours and material cost tables—which included all items involved in HVAC piping and sheet metal, and plumbing systems, all broken down to the degree needed for plus or minus a one or two percent accuracy.

My consulting engineering and software development firm reached an acceptable plateau in the first half of the 1990s, and then it was time to retire in 1996. I was ready to take a rest from the industry.

Conducted Seminars Nationwide

In addition to being a software developer in the later 1970s and '80s, construction was booming and seminars were hot. So, after over 20 years of actual experience in the HVAC field with Mellish and

Murray, and being an instructor and article-writer on various HVAC topics, it led to the opportunity to conduct seminars nationwide on my own.

I conducted four different HVAC seminars around the country for 13 years, from 1977 to about 1990. The seminars were popular in the U.S. during those busy construction years. The first seminar was on estimating, the second on testing and balancing HVAC systems, the third on energy conservation, and the fourth covered a new energy-efficient HVAC system called "variable volume."

I launched the first seminar and called it "Everything You Ever Wanted to Know About Sheet Metal Estimating But Were Afraid to Ask." It was based on my development of the more accurate systems of estimating ductwork, and "The Eight Facets of the Estimating Diamond."

I wrote the copy for a four-page brochure to advertise the estimating seminar. It was mailed to about six Midwestern states, about 6,000 brochures. The first one was in Chicago. The estimating seminar was the most successful one, along with testing and balancing seminars launched later. Not only was preparing better estimates for bidding in vogue then, but there also was a big swing to testing and balancing HVAC systems, and it became a booming new requirement of most larger building projects. The other two seminars did fairly well, but were not as popular.

I hired a high school graphic artist, Dianne, the daughter of a good friend of ours, who designed the artwork for the estimating and testing and balancing seminars brochures. Later, she went to college and got a degree in graphic arts, and worked for various companies in a graphic artist's capacity.

Along with the seminars, I wrote companion books to go with each seminar as I went along. All four were published on the topics of estimating, testing and balancing, energy conservation, and variable air volume systems. Some of the books are still selling on the market.

When I retired in 1996, I sold my firm to Joe in Boston, who was handling our software sales, along with his sheet metal fabrication machinery and software for three years. They are still a major player in the field.

Chapter 19

SQUEEZING IN WRITING TIME

My writing career started in 1937 when I was seven years old in the second grade at Fiske Elementary School on the south side of Chicago. I wrote a poem called "Trees," which was put in the school newspaper.

The next venture in writing was at Lane Tech High School in Chicago where, as a freshman in 1945, I wrote articles for the school newspaper. The hankering to write became apparent at this time. Squeezing it in and making it happen was a problem. After graduating from high school, I studied short story writing, which was more popular back in those days, and wrote several stories. Not much happened with them. Later, when I was married and a father of four, this ambition of story writing faded away.

As a member of an engineering society, I wrote the newsletter for our Chicago ASHRAE chapter. This was when I was working with Mellish and Murray. I also wrote another newsletter for HVAC contractors when I was conducting estimating seminars around the country.

I also wrote poems for greeting cards for birthdays, holidays, and other special occasions for my wife, relatives, and friends. Wrote them also for readings at the different writers' clubs I belonged to in the Chicago and Phoenix areas, and wrote prayers for special occasions. These were minor writing ventures.

Bigger writing projects, however, followed when I resigned from Mellish and Murray and opened up my consultant engineering company. I wrote five technical manuals, which were used with my nationwide seminars I conducted in the later 1970s and 1980s. The books and seminars covered HVAC topics, estimating costs, testing and balancing systems, conserving energy, and so on.

Despite full-time work, long driving time to and from work, having four kids, and attending college at night, I squeezed in writing time. I wrote about a dozen HVAC magazine articles such as: "Your Chance to STAR"; "The Eight Facets of the Estimating Diamond"; "Fifteen Orphans with No Regular Homes" (referring to construction specification items that bounce around), and more.

Christmas Plays

My talented granddaughter Megan and I wrote several Christmas plays together in the early 2000s. The plays were written for my grandchildren to present at the family's Christmas Eve get-together at my younger brother's house.

Together, we would conceive what the play would be about, work out the storyline, and come up with character names, some dialogue, and the settings. I then typed the scripts for the plays. *The Digital Clock Fairy* was the title of the first play. Amelia and Mr. Bailey were middle-aged neighbor friends in a small town in Illinois. They both longed to find where their grandparents lived in Germany, and they planned a surprise visit to them around Christmastime. The Digital Clock Fairy helps make their wishes magically come true. The fairy also helps the grandmother of Mr. Bailey to make a remarkable discovery.

The second Christmas play for the kids, *The Queen's Lost Doll*, took them to England, where they helped the queen find her lost doll and a missing 50-karat diamond, which was stuffed in the doll.

The third play took the grandchildren to England once more. They got an invitation to a Christmas dinner at Buckingham Palace with the queen and family to honor them for finding the queen's doll and diamond. The visit almost doesn't happen because of problems, but the character Megan portrays in the play saves the day.

The fourth and last production with the grandchildren was titled *The Reason for the Season; In Search of the True Meaning of Christmas,* where each grandchild tried to come up with the real reason, but failed, whereas the youngest came up with a surprising answer.

Another area of tough technical writing was in my consulting engineering firm where we developed and sold two large software programs. I wrote and revised our software instruction manuals, which was a major headache—a never-ending series of new manuals and revisions. Each time we graduated from an older computer to an updated model, or upgraded our software, or revised because of advancements in operating systems and computer writing languages, I had to revise or even completely rewrite the instruction manuals. This involved a great deal of sweat and time, because of a constantly changing industry and products.

The Essential Elements of *Making Four-Star Decisions: Reorganizing Your Brain Cells*

I wrote an instruction manual titled *Making Four-Star Decisions: Reorganizing Your Brain Cells,* as a supplement to the seminars I conducted and for my employees.

Four-Star Decisions is about creating better solutions and making smarter decisions in your life—at home, at work, socially, and in worldly matters. It's about how to solve life's problems better, from the bassinette to the casket. Success in your personal life, at work, in business, and in government is tied directly to how effectively you solve your problems and make decisions. Four-Star Decisions mean happiness, confidence, and achievements in your life by meeting your goals. It means controlling your mental processes and misleading impulses and emotions.

The pursuit of the Four-Star Decision all started when I began to figure out how to overcome some of my inferiority and anxiety feelings built up in my childhood life. As I progressed in this pursuit, I began to improve my overall behavior and self-worth image. I began to reorganize my brains cells in the problem-solving, decision-making process.

When I encountered difficult problems, and feelings and thoughts of inferiority started to make me feel negative or incompetent, I began by asking myself, "Just what is the problem?" I thought about what the requirements of the solution were, which are the goals and objectives that the option chosen must satisfy. I would ask myself, "What options are available and what are the effects of these options?" As I progressed along these lines, I continually made more accurate and informed decisions.

I researched and studied what had been developed and written in the past on problem solving and decision making from the Greek philosophers Plato, Socrates, and Aristotle to John Dewey, who wrote *How We Think*. I examined their valid concepts and techniques and gave them due consideration and attention. What was not that effective and hadn't proven itself was discounted; or where it needed to be updated, I did so.

It didn't all just fall into place or become a smooth process overnight; it took years and years to put all the phases and principles together and to be skilled at applying the process. Over the years the techniques were tested over and over and have proven to work. They have been streamlined and polished for maximum effectiveness.

Today I can just about guarantee that if the "absolute requirements" concept is applied, along with identifying the problem accurately and identifying all the options and checking them against the absolute requirements, you will make remarkable decisions and avoid the careless or dumb ones.

Part V

NEIGHBORING TREES AND
FELLOW BRANCHES

Chapter 20
STORIES ABOUT MY NEXT OF KIN

My Immediate Family

My mother went through many tough and some tragic times in her life. To start with, she was born and raised as an orphan in poverty in Germany in the early 1900s. After coming to America, she suffered in the breakup with her first husband. There were some difficult years with my stepfather in the 1940s, then, when she was older, her foster mother died. Near the end of life she suffered a stroke and lived out her life in a nursing home. In spite of all this, she was a trooper and a survivor.

An Orphan's Life in Old Germany

The midwife slapped Rose's newborn posterior on August 28, 1909 in a bedroom in Schneidhain, a small town in central Germany near Frankfort. Rose broke out crying. The midwife said the father could come in now. However, the father was not there. He was out of town, but no one knew where. They weren't even sure of his name. It was Ludwig or maybe Erick. They settled on Ludwig as the name of the wandering, philandering, rogue, runaway father and salesman.

Rose's mother, Katrina Gottschalk, was sickly and had complications with the birth. She did not recover and two months after Rose's birth she died. This was the beginning of my mother's orphan life with no mother, nor apparently a father to take care of her.

Rose's grandparents said they would help out in the beginning for a little while until a home was found for Rose, but they were not ready or willing to raise the child full-time. Some months later they found a place for the baby Rose, and she went to live with a close friend of her mother's, Leni Anglebrandt, who had one child, a 10-year-old daughter.

After a few years the arrangement with the friend of Rose's mother wasn't working well and Rose went to live with her mother's brother and his wife. Rose didn't like the aunt, but she liked her uncle. Unfortunately, he was killed in the First World War. Things got worse. Rose wanted to leave and the aunt wanted her to move out.

Rosa, 8 years old, 1917 in Germany

My mother Rosa in Germany, an eight-year-old orphan

Rose's Foster Parents

At the same time that Rose was dealing with the death of her uncle in about 1920, 200 miles north in the town of Bremerhaven Rose's father, Ludwig, met a woman named Emma, who knew nothing about Ludwig, nothing about the fact that he was a runaway and a philandering father. She didn't realize he was a ladies' man and after a brief courting, Emma fell for him and they got married. He gave no indication about his past life and his illegitimate daughter.

However, after some time in the marriage, Emma discovered he had a daughter who lived in the Frankfurt area. The irresponsible, sordid situation that had occurred was revealed to Emma. She found out that he left town and disappeared after the birth; that he did nothing to help Rose; and that the orphan Rose was shuffled around from grandparents, to a neighbor, and to an aunt.

Emma was horrified over the revelations about Ludwig. She insisted that Ludwig do something to rectify the situation. She told him that he must go down to Frankfort and bring his daughter back to Bremerhaven to live with them. He agreed and left Bremerhaven for Frankfort, alone, apparently with that intent. But, somewhere along the way to Frankfurt he must have gotten waylaid with drinking and chasing women. He never got there and never returned to Bremerhaven. Emma waited and waited. She finally checked with the aunt, and found out that Ludwig never showed up and nobody knew where he was.

Emma became disillusioned and disgusted with Ludwig and had the marriage annulled. However, she felt sorry for Rose's plight and went down to the Frankfort area herself to meet Rose and find out how things were going. She found out the uncle was dead, and that the aunt was poor and had little or nothing to give Rose. The aunt could just barely feed her own daughter and herself.

Emma saw the pathetic conditions that Rose was living in, but found Rose to be a wonderful, beautiful, and intelligent child, despite the turmoil in her life. Emma couldn't contain herself. She fell in love with Rose, and felt deep sympathy for this pretty young girl with a sullen look. She wanted to take her back to Bremerhaven and be her foster mother, but she hadn't the means to do so at that time.

Before Emma left Frankfurt to go back to Bremerhaven she bought Rose some new clothes. She told the aunt of her intent to be

Rose's foster mother and that she would help the aunt out with the expenses of taking care of Rose until she was able to bring her to Bremerhaven. Emma went back home and continued with her work and life, saving as much as she could. She wrote Rose and the aunt often, checking on Rose's well-being.

While Emma was back home again in Bremerhaven, she met another man, William Keller, who was working in the theater as a magician, hypnotist, and illusionist. William was a kind, thoughtful man with unusual talents. They fell in love and got married in about 1921. Emma told William beforehand about her disastrous marriage to Ludwig, and about the orphan Rose in the Frankfurt area. Because Emma and Willy found out that they were unable to have children, William agreed to take Rose in as a foster child. Emma made arrangements to do so. Rose was about 12 years old at that time in 1921, and they brought her to Bremerhaven.

They raised Rose as unofficial foster parents for about four years, from about the age of 12 to 16. Nothing more was heard or seen of Ludwig again.

In 1925, when Rose was 16 years old, a brother of William Keller's, who had immigrated to Chicago, offered to sponsor William and Emma to do the same. The brother officially committed to getting William a job, and for being responsible for both of them— but he did not offer to sponsor Rose. Willy and Emma decided to make the move to Chicago while they had a chance, anyway.

Rose Immigrates to America

Emma and William left Rose in Bremerhaven and planned to wait until they were situated enough in America to sponsor her. Rose wanted to join the theater but Emma nixed it. They found a job for her in Bremerhaven at a Catholic home for retired seaman. Someone in the seamen's home wrote Emma, who was now in the U.S., and recommended sending Rose to a convent home. Emma rejected this and decided to sponsor Rose and bring her over to live with them sooner rather than later.

Rose immigrated in 1926 at about the age of 17. She was quite attractive as a young woman, had a nice smile, a strong body, firm muscles, and was a hard worker. Her mouth was a little narrow and came to a bit of a point; however, the upper front teeth did not stick out. They just formed a pointed arch and made it difficult to smile with her lips closed.

She took an ocean liner across the Atlantic, landed at Ellis Island and passed the physical and other requirements. On the train going from New York to Chicago she met some German men and sang Christmas songs with them.

Mother, 26, emigrated from Bremerhaven to the U.S. in 1927 at the age of 17 to be with her foster parents on the south side.

Rose Meets My Father

My maternal father, Carl Wendes, was born in Nossen, Germany, near Dresden in 1901. Carl's parents, Clara and Theodore Wendes, had five children; Carl, who was the youngest of those who survived; and his two older sisters, Johanna and Elizabeth also

189

survived. The other two children that Carl's parents had were fraternal twins named Edith and Herbert. Edith was a blue baby and lived three weeks. Herbert died of whooping cough at age two, about a year later. Carl's father, Theodore Wendes, born in 1869, died of diabetes in 1918 at the age of 49. He was buried in Altfeld, Germany, making Carl's mother Clara a widow.

While Carl was growing up, the family moved from Nossen, near the Elba River in the eastern part of Germany, to Altfeld, in the northwest part of Germany. Then in 1923, after the First World War, times were tough and runaway inflation was so bad in Germany that Carl decided to immigrate to the U.S. with his mother, Clara, and oldest sister, Elizabeth, to the land of plenty and opportunity. The younger sister Johanna stayed in Germany because I believe she was engaged to August Heinrich, whom she married later.

Upon arriving in Chicago, Carl got a job with Spiegel's, a merchandising company. His first home was on 58th street near Cottage Grove, near the University of Chicago and Midway Park on the south side of Chicago. These grounds were in the area of the White City World's Fair of 1893.

Some time later he moved to the north side of Chicago and took a job as a janitor, even though he was a tool and die maker by trade in Germany. The job was in a large, three-story apartment building on Fullerton and Kedzie near Logan Square in Chicago. Carl's mother and sister, who were living with him on 58th Street, moved into the janitor's apartment with Carl. The sunken apartment, which was provided with the job, was half below ground level and half above.

Romance, Marriage, Problems

While living in the janitor's apartment in 1927, Carl's mother Clara met some neighbors, Willy and Emma Keller, who had emigrated from Germany the year before. Clara and Emma Keller often talked when they bumped into each other when buying fresh rolls for breakfast in the morning. Clara and Emma became friends as they talked about Germany and life in America.

Rosa and Carl Wendes marry, early 1928

My mother and paternal father's wedding picture

Emma told her about her now 18-year-old foster child, Rose, who they had recently sponsored to immigrate to the U.S. and who was now living with them. Clara told Emma about her son, 26-year-old Carl, who lived with her.

Carl's mother invited the Kellers and Rose to dinner so that Carl and Rose could meet. They met and were attracted to each other. Carl courted her for some time and they got married in January of 1928. My mother moved in with my father in the janitor's apartment, so

Carl's mother Clara and his sister and family, the Heinrichs, who were still living with him at the time, had to move out.

Rose and Carl had their first child, Rudolph William Theodore Wendes, a nice long name, in November of 1928. I was born a little over 2 ½ years later in 1931. My younger half brother arrived on the scene about six years later.

Carl was a shorter, slightly slim man, but whose proportions were just right. He also had a way of looking at you while thinking about what he was going to say and giving you a friendly smile at the same time. You could see the gears working in his brain. After this pause his lips would quiver a bit and he would come out with a carefully worded, thoughtful statement. People liked him. But even though his life in the U.S. started out brightly, full of hope, his ultimate family life got goofed up. He became disappointed and frustrated and then he drank too much at times.

Clara never learned much English. A German nickname for "grandmother" in Germany was Oma, pronounced *oh-mah*. But she never learned or spoke much English and somehow the German nickname got changed to *amu*, pronounced *ah-moo*. Once it got started that way it stuck until she died. Clara was of the old German culture—humble, responsible, and she just did her duties quietly and pleasantly.

Paternal father Carl with two older sisters
Johanna and Elizabeth in Germany

One Stupid Drink Too Much

Rose and Carl lived in the janitor's apartment for many years, giving birth to Rudy and me. The honeymoon phase of my parents' marriage faded. The stark reality of life for immigrants in America in the Depression years in a coal-burning apartment building was disappointing. Their lifestyles, as husband, wife, and parents, didn't match up as they hoped. It brought frustration to their marriage.

A threatening affair happened one night. It occurred in 1935, when I was four, my older brother Rudy was six, and my mother 26.

My father and some drinking buddies of his got boisterous in the kitchen of the apartment. They were drinking boilermakers, a combination of a beer and a shot of schnapps or whiskey, which was customary in those days. He and his crony friends were going at it for hours into the middle of the night. My mother couldn't sleep nor stand the noise anymore. I woke up from the noise and started crying. Rudy woke up and whined about the noise and asked my mother what was wrong.

This wasn't the first time the group had used our kitchen for their drinking bashes. It had happened before. After these late-night drinking romps, my father wouldn't get up at five a.m. the next morning to stoke up the cinders in the boiler and shovel in new coal. Consequently, on these mornings when he didn't get up, it was left to my dutiful mother to do this janitorial work for him. She had to get up at five, dress, go into the boiler room behind our basement apartment, and stoke and shovel in new coal.

On that night, she finally got out of bed at one or two o'clock to put a stop to the raucous behavior. She went into the kitchen and angrily demanded his drinking buddies leave. After they left, my mother started hollering at my father and they got into an explosive argument. "Stop your drinking and stop bringing your boozing friends into our apartment for half the night!" In his drunken and angry state, he made a threatening remark that he might end things for all of us.

My mother became a bit frantic. She was struck with fear. As a measure of caution she wanted to make sure nothing bad happened to Rudy and me. With a presence of mind to protect herself and her two boys, despite her terror, she ran and got the .45 automatic pistol my father kept in the top drawer of a dresser, and tossed it into the boiler right behind our janitor's apartment.

She got on the phone and called her foster mother, who was living on the south side of Chicago, and told her about the horrible situation. Her foster mother told my mother to call the police right away and that she and William would be there as quickly as possible.

The police were there in minutes and my father was shocked into some sobriety. They took down all the information, and told both my mother and father to sit down and calm down. They waited patiently for my mother's foster parents to arrive.

It was decided that my mother and Rudy and I would leave Carl that very night and move in with the Kellers, and not stay another day with my father. My mother, as far as I knew, didn't want to charge Carl with anything and didn't even understand the procedure. The police stayed until my mother packed as much as she could. She then went with the Kellers, taking Rudy and me to the south side of Chicago to live with them.

From One Janitor's Apartment to Another

My mother's foster father, Willy, was also a janitor living in a small janitor's apartment with only one bedroom in a big, three-story, 24-flat building, They converted the living room into a bedroom for my mother, Rudy and me. The conditions were cramped. Big steam and water pipes ran exposed through the room along the ceiling. It felt funny when I lay in bed at night and looked up at them. I could hear the water gurgling through the pipes and I hoped they wouldn't leak on my bed.

There was some talk that there was more than drinking behind the frustration that burst out that night on Fullerton Avenue. My mother was young when she married Carl, about 18. He was eight years older. She liked to go dancing in the local school hall. He went with her reluctantly, and as was the custom in Germany in those days, they danced with other strange men, and not just with their partners.

When they had a dance contest one night at the school hall, she desperately wanted to go, but Carl refused, so she went alone. She hooked up with some other guy—maybe she knew him already from previous dances—and they won first prize. When Carl found out about it he was infuriated, jealous, and hurt. This may have been a major disturbing factor in their marriage.

We lived with the Kellers in the janitor's apartment for about a year and a half. What ensued then was peculiar. My estranged father kept on going to see my mother at the foster grandparents' apartment and pleading with her to come back to him. He still loved her. He promised to quit drinking, and so on, but my mother was too scared from the trauma to take a chance and would not go back. After a while it became disturbing to Rose, so Emma told Carl emphatically to stop trying to see her.

What brought finality to their marriage and divorce (in Carl's mind) was that a friend of the Kellers introduced Rose to Paul Neuhauser, Sr. After some appropriate amount of time, they courted and were married. This part of the story about my mother's second marriage to Paul is covered in the next chapter, 21, about step-relatives.

When my mother left Carl he told her that if she didn't come back in two years, he would marry another woman with two boys the same age as Rudy and me. And indeed, Carl did marry another woman, Catherine, exactly two years later. And she did have two boys, Robert and Alvin, each the same ages as Rudy and me. Bob was six days older than Rudy, and Al was 12 days younger than me. My father's prophecy came true.

During the two-year period between my father's divorce in 1935 and his remarriage to Catherine in 1937, Carl's sister Johanna and her new family moved back in with him in the Fullerton janitor's apartment. This was the second time that the Heinrichs moved in with Carl on Fullerton, but this time it was with two children; Fred, born in 1932; and Lucille, born in September, 1935—two wonderful, quick to laugh with you, intelligent cousins. I also liked their mother, a cheerful, considerate person, who was my aunt and godmother.

When Carl remarried in 1937, and his new wife Catherine and two boys moved in with him, the Heinrichs had to go through the revolving door and move out again.

Custody and Visitations

The divorce judge decreed my mother to have custody of my brother and me, but we were directed to visit my father every other weekend. The first years Carl picked us up regularly on Friday afternoons and brought us back on Sunday afternoons. After a while he slacked off and it would be called off more often than not. Sometimes he called my mother to let her know he wasn't going to make it. Sometimes he wouldn't call at all. We would only know the visitation was going to take place when he came late to pick us up.

Then, after a number of years, he didn't call at all until Rudy and I were old enough to go there on our own. We would then take the elevated train by ourselves to visit him and stay over Friday and Saturday nights. We would drive Catherine a little nuts as we romped through the house with her two boys. Our visits lasted until we were 18 years old.

In the 1950s, as we became young adults, my brother and I would visit our father only on holidays, birthdays, and when we felt like it. We also managed to visit our aunts, the Heinrich and Staib families, at times. We enjoyed seeing our cousins, Fred and Lucille Heinrich and Carl Staib.

My paternal father kept on drinking off and on through the years in his marriage with Catherine. She adored him and they got along. However, he often became belligerent when he drank too much. When at a local tavern, he would start to argue with someone, get mad and start a fight with them. A few times he ended up getting thrown in jail. Then he would call his brother-in-law, August Heinrich, in the middle of the night to come to the station to post bail and get him out. August, a more proper and dignified gentleman, did so, but I don't think he liked to do it. It must have bothered him to go to the police station and make bail. He probably felt obligated to do so because Carl had helped him to immigrate here.

Mother Lost Herself in Work

After Rose married her second husband Paul, and had her third boy, she got more used to things in the U.S. and became a hard worker. But she didn't seem fully happy because of some of the arguing and fighting with Paul, and she lost herself in her work as a cover-up. She was not afraid of work; she was fast, and it gave her great satisfaction. She could wash the kitchen floor in minutes—and it was clean. She dusted furniture and vacuumed carpets with great

197

gusto. Walls in the house had to be washed or painted frequently because of the coal-burning furnaces. She was a whiz at washing windows and did so often. She could hang laundry outside in minutes. I think she was secretly glad that a housewife's work is never done. She could walk miles at a fast clip, even in her upper 70s.

She cleaned other people's houses and apartments about three times a week and was sought after. She arrived a little early in the morning and drank a cup of coffee with the tenants first. Then she zipped through most of the cleaning, which was done very well, by lunchtime. After lunch she got through the balance of work an hour earlier than what was expected. She then had coffee and cake with the tenants again, got paid, and usually left by three o'clock.

Rose loved her three boys more than anything in her life. She was terribly proud of them. They grew up under her guidance, had families, grandchildren, and success in their lives—more than she ever dreamed, having had the tough, humble childhood for years as an orphan and living a lot of the time in poverty.

My mother was very close and dependent on her foster mother Emma from after her divorce in 1935 until 1960. Problems developed after her foster father died in 1960. Emma was forlorn without her husband, and she passed away soon after in the same year. She sort of blamed Rose for tying herself to Emma too much and causing some of the sorrow after William died.

After Emma died, Rose continued her housecleaning work two or three days a week for a number of years. In December of 1971 my stepfather died from cancer of the lungs at the age of 64. My mother, 59 at the time, stayed in the brick bi-level house in Des Plaines and managed it on her own the next 14 years. She kept the house spotless, planted flowers in spring, did her shopping, and rented out a bedroom to tenants, mainly women.

And one of the big things she did was cook tasty German dinners for her three sons and their families nearly every Sunday. These dinners included such items as potato dumplings, pork roasts, lots of gravy, and homemade chicken soup. We could see the circles of fat floating on the surface of the soup, and savored the dark brown gravy laden with fat, but it tasted oh so good!

Around 1985 my mother suffered a tiny stroke and then a big one. She became confined to a wheelchair, her talking became a little slurred and she never could walk again. My two brothers and I hired full-time nurses to take care of her. Living became very difficult. She couldn't get in and out of bed, go to the washroom herself, or dress herself. So, we decided to put her in a nursing home in Rolling Meadows, IL, where she survived for a few more years.

When I visited her there she often asked in a despondent and helpless tone, "When will I walk again and get out of the wheelchair?" She could hardly stand, much less walk. Finally, she lost hope, gave up eating and drinking liquids for two weeks and passed away on August 4th, 1992. She was three weeks shy of her 83rd birthday. She would have been 104 if she were alive today in 2013.

Chapter 21
AUNTS AND UNCLES ON
FATHER'S SIDE

The Heinrichs

In the beginning, my paternal father, Carl Wendes, was very happy and excited to be living in the New World in 1923. After several years in Chicago, he wrote a letter to his sister, Johanna, in Germany urging her to move here with her fiancé, August Heinrich. Carl, his sister Elizabeth, and his mother Clara had been in the U.S. for four years already, but the other sister, Johanna, hadn't made up her mind yet to come here. Carl, who had not met my mother yet, wrote that he would sponsor his sister Johanna and her fiancé.

He told Johanna and August that he would send them money for transportation and that they could stay with him until August found work and could support them. He detailed everything they should do, what to take with them, how to handle the voyage from Germany to America, what to say and not say on Ellis Island, and how to get on the train to come to Chicago.

It was a very intelligent and helpful letter. There would be no hurry to pay him back. Carl also related how he had constructed his own crystal radio, which could tune in Germany and other countries. He was proud of the new technology in the New World.

August had wanted to move to South America, but Johanna wanted to move close to her family in Chicago and she prevailed. So, Carl's sister Johanna married August in Germany and then immigrated here in 1927. They lived with Carl and their mother Clara on 58th Street above a Piggly Wiggly store on the south side of Chicago. When Carl married my mother Rose in January of 1928, he moved into the janitor's apartment on Fullerton Avenue. The Heinrichs and Clara stayed in the apartment on 58th Street.

Johanna and August had two children; Fred, born in 1933 and Lucille, born in 1935, who were two wonderful cousins. Johanna was my godmother. She was a generous, cheerful, kind woman, but also calmly serious about things and knew well what she was doing. The cousins took on her cheerful personality and it was always fun to see them, both when we were kids and later as adults.

Fred served in the service around 1951 and then married Alice in 1953, and together they had five children. Lucille married Carl Scharf, who had a doctorate degree in horticulture and was a teacher in a Chicago Teacher's College. Together they had four daughters.

The Staibs

In 1926 my father's oldest sister, Elizabeth, married Chris Staib, a baker in Chicago. She subsequently moved out of my father's apartment on Fullerton to live with her husband. They had one child, my cousin Carl Staib, in 1927. My grandmother, Clara, who had been living with her sister Johanna, moved in with the Staibs after Johanna had their second child.

The Staibs bought and lived in a two-story apartment building in Oak Park some years later. They had a giant, ferocious German Shepherd dog that would put me in a panic. When I visited them, the dog gave out a continuous, ear-crackling bellow and looked like it would lunge at my throat. I am sure it would have if my aunt hadn't restrained the monster and put him in a bedroom. However, he would keep on barking in the bedroom all the time I was there and the walls would vibrate.

My cousin, Carl Staib, lived alone in the Oak Park apartment after his parents and grandmother died. He retired from his union printing job as a pressman. He never married. His other aunt, Johanna, who was a widow then, moved in with him after her husband died, presumably to save some money on rent, and take care of him because of his bad eyesight. He wore super thick glasses. She lived with him until she died some years later.

He Became a Hoarder

After his Aunt Johanna died, Carl became a hermit, living alone. He ordered pizza and beer and had it delivered to his apartment regularly. He threw the empty pizza boxes and beer cans everywhere in the apartment while he watched television from morning to night. He became what we know today as a hoarder. He didn't put the empty containers in garbage bags or bring them outside for garbage pickup. Eventually, the piles of junk grew and grew and got higher and higher and one could hardly see over the mountains of trash or find one's way to the bathroom.

During this period when Carl lived alone, his close cousins, Fred and Lucille Heinrich, visited occasionally and tried to get Carl to clean things up. But it didn't help much because Carl disregarded their pleas and continued to litter up the apartment with pizza boxes and beer cans.

Finally, Carl died, leaving the garbage and stench behind for his two cousins, Fred and Lucille, to clean up. But that wasn't the big problem following his death. Carl didn't have a will, so the two-story apartment building in Oak Park that he inherited and lived in, went into probate. Fred and Lucille, who cared for Carl and the apartment building for years, felt that they should inherit the building under the circumstances. They put their claim in, but "no way" said the judge, who decreed since there was no will and no obvious surviving immediate family, other potential relatives in the U.S. and Europe had to be contacted to see if they had claims.

It took years to go through probate and it ended up that several obscure cousins on the father's side in Poland laid claim to the inheritance. When it all started the building was in good shape and could have been sold for a good amount. By the time the whole probate was finished the building was in shambles—virtually worth nothing. Fred and Lucille said they were frustrated and greatly disappointed.

Hidden Aunt and Uncle, Revealed

My brother Rudy and I, and our cousins, could have had another aunt and uncle in our lives. I didn't know about it until recently. While reviewing notes and letters on my ancestors for my memoirs, I came across some information in a letter written by my cousin's daughter.

I discovered that my paternal grandparents in Germany, Clara and Theodore Wendes, not only had three children, as most of us believed, but they actually had two more children, for a total of five.

In 1908 my grandmother, Clara, gave birth to fraternal twins, a boy and a girl, in Okreftel, Germany. They were the latest and last births of the children, the births of the first three siblings occurring many years earlier. The girl's name was Edith Wendes and the boy's name was Herbert Wendes.

Edith, a blue baby, died three weeks after birth and Herbert died of whooping cough at two. A blue baby is one who is born with bluish skin usually because of a heart defect. Fraternal twins are born of separate ova and are not identical.

We can ponder about the grief my grandparents probably went through, let our imaginations create a picture of their lives at that time, and feel empathy for them. But in any case, medical technology was not there yet to help them out; no vaccinations, heart surgery, or penicillin.

But, we can also amuse ourselves by dreaming of what pleasures we may have had knowing the twins, had they lived and immigrated to the U.S. as their other three siblings did.

During the last years of my paternal father's life in the 1960s, Carl cut down his drinking and worked for Western Electric in Chicago as a tool and die maker. He died in Chicago in December 1972 at the age of 71. The turmoil, frustrations, and disappointments didn't need to be drowned out anymore by occasional drinking in a Chicago bar and starting a fight with guys bigger than him.

On left, my wife's cousin Kathi with husband, Werner. On right, sister-in-law Rosemary and my wife. In Heidenheim near Ulm.

Chapter 22
STEP-RELATIVES FROM SECOND MARRIAGES

My Stepfather, Paul Neuhauser, Sr.

After my parents divorced in 1935, my mother, older brother and I were stuffed into a cramped three-room janitor's apartment with the Kellers on the south side of Chicago. Their living room became a temporary bedroom for us. After about a year and a half living under these conditions, the Kellers heard about a young single German man, Paul Neuhauser, Sr., from a tenant in the Kellers' apartment building. They made arrangements for my mother to meet him.

Paul was born in Bavaria, Germany and immigrated to Chicago in 1934 because of tough economic conditions in Germany in the 1930s. He left his home, where he lived with his sister Elizabeth and mother Elisa Neuhauser in Emmering, a small town near Munich. Paul's father, Georg Neuhauser, died mountain climbing in the Alps in a snow storm in 1921 at the age of 59. Elisa died in 1941 at 76.

The first cold winter Paul was in Chicago in early 1934, before he had a permanent place to live, he slept on a streetcar on Western Avenue during cold nights. It was well heated and you could stay on it as long as you wanted with one fare. It was the longest street in Chicago, a straight street going from one end of the city to the other for about 25 miles.

When he was introduced to my mother, Paul worked as a bartender at the Bismark, an upscale hotel where the Chicago politicians hung out in downtown Chicago. He also sold greeting cards to people he met bartending and did well at it. Paul was personable, knew how to talk to and treat the politicians, and had a broad smile. He was a bit short, maybe five-feet two-inches, but nevertheless was a little taller than Rose. He was neat and well dressed.

Paul courted Rose, they fell in love, and got married in 1936. We moved out of the overcrowded Keller apartment, and moved to the third floor of a three-story apartment building on Maryland Avenue. It had no elevators and it was tough walking up three flights of stairs. We lived there for a year or two and then moved into another three-story brick building, but this time on the first floor. It was on Engleside Avenue, a half a block away from the Kellers.

On November 24th in 1937 my mother and stepfather had a healthy baby boy, my younger half brother Paul George Neuhauser, Jr.

My mother also yearned yet to have a daughter. But a later pregnancy with my stepfather, in the middle 1940s, ended up with a still birth; the baby strangled itself on the umbilical cord. Ironically, it was a girl. Even though Paul tried to hide the fact that it was a girl and told her it was a boy, she never believed it.

Despite some difficulties in the early years of my mother and stepfather's marriage (as described in Chapter 8, "Tough Family Years"), I loved my stepfather. He was a dedicated, hard-working, generous man and I believe he loved not only his son, Paul, but also my older brother and me. I have the same gratitude for him for the success in our lives as I do for my mother.

Emmering, the Bierlings, and Oels

Back in Emmering, Germany, Paul's sister Elizabeth married a gentleman named Hans Bierling, Sr., who was the rector of a school. After WWII ended in 1945, we sent food and clothing packages to them. They had three children, Gertraud, Fred, and Hans, Jr. One of the sons, Fred, was married twice and died an untimely death. The daughter married Josef Oel and they had two boys, Hans and

Werner. Elizabeth's other son, Hans, Jr. married Angelica and had two sons.

When I was in the service stationed in Germany in 1954, Hanna and I visited Paul's sister Elizabeth, and the daughter, Gertraud, and her fiancé, Josef Oel. We were graciously and warmly welcomed. My wife and I got to know them well and we became friends over the years.

After I was out of the service and back in the United States we made numerous visits to Germany. The first time we went back to Emmering was with our four children in 1971, and we visited my stepfather's sister and the Gertraud Oels family, who lived together then. By that time Gertraud and her husband Josef had been married for some time and had the two growing boys, Hans and Werner.

Hans Oel married Heike, a very friendly, energetic and likeable person. They have three splendid children, Christian, Katherina, and Florian. Werner Oel, Hans's brother, married Hannelore and they have four nice children, Magdalena, Sebastian, Verena, and Tobia.

Hans and Heike and family in Augsburg area in recent years

207

Heike and the children also came to visit us in the United States during different years. Paul's sister and Hans Jr. came first in the later 1950s. Hans Jr., with his wife Angelica, visited us here in the 1970s. The Oels and their children, Christian, Katherina, and Florian, came to visit us more in the early 2000s. Whenever we met, whether in the United States or Germany, they were always happy, fun occasions. They are a wonderful group of good-looking people, and we became friends over the years.

Stepbrothers, Bob and Al

The other step-relatives I have were through a second marriage of my paternal father, Carl, in 1936. As I related in the last chapter, my father married Catherine after he divorced my mother. She had two boys from her previous marriage the same age as my older brother Rudy and myself.

Al and Bob, Catherine's two boys, subsequently grew up with my father, their new stepfather, and their mother. They had some problems in their adult years, which I am not too familiar with, but they seemed to straighten things out as they got older. Carl and Catherine lived in Chicago near Belmont and Lincoln Avenues, and later in a two-story house set way back on a lot on Austin Boulevard. After Carl died she moved to Pontiac, IL where her youngest son Al was living. She was born in 1910 and died in Pontiac, IL in 1982 at the age of 72.

Al's and Bob's adult lives were sketchy to me after the visitation rights to my father ended. They left home and got married, so they were not around when we made occasional visits to my father. Al worked at horse racetracks and traveled around the country. He got married and had, I believe, two daughters, one named Carla. In later years, Al worked at the jail in Pontiac as a guard until he retired. He was born in 1931 and died in May of 1999 at the age of 67 and was cremated. Carla still lives and works in Pontiac with her son and daughter.

Bob had some fine artistic abilities, but ended up working as a tool and die maker at machine shops in Illinois and California. He was married twice. He had two daughters, Theresa and Cynthia, by his first marriage with Betty in the 1950s. Bob married his second wife, Kathleen, in 1968 and they had two sons.

Bob lived in a northern suburb of Chicago for many years until he died in 2008. He was afflicted with a number of health problems as he got older; diabetes, diverticulitis, sclerosis of the liver, and emphysema.

Chapter 23
FRIENDS OVER THE YEARS

The Gang

It was a sunny afternoon in 2012 when we met outside the Chicago Brauhaus restaurant on Lincoln Avenue. The old gang was waiting outside for us, and starting to take pictures when my wife and I walked around the corner from the parking lot. They waved us over and we joined the group of a dozen friends. "Hello, how are you? Good to see you again." It was a jovial, friendly get-together. We talked a little, took a couple group pictures, and then went into the restaurant. These are the people I have known since our early school years over 70 years ago.

The Brauhaus was a large restaurant with genuine German flair. Relic ornamental beer steins were displayed on shelves, all the beams and columns were a darker wood, and in one corner was a dance floor where a man played the accordion. The food was genuine German cooking, plus German beers on tap. We felt like we were in old Germany.

It may have appeared that we were meeting with some of our German friends who immigrated to the United States, but we were not. It was the gang from Chicago that I grew up with. Our group has met for lunches a few times a year at different restaurants for years. Prior to meeting at restaurants, we got together for weekends in places like Door County in Wisconsin. In the 1960s and '70s we would meet wherever Dave had his boat docked, picnic on the boat, and then take a cruise on Lake Michigan.

When we were seated in the Brauhaus, the waitress asked each of us, "Would you like something to drink?" Most of us ordered a half a stein of German beer on tap. When she got to Herb, she asked, "What would you like, Herbie?"

He looked up at the waitress and said in a serious, but friendly way, "I'm not a Herbie, I'm a Herb. Herbie is for little kids."

The waitress, afraid she might have offended him, answered, "Oh, I'm so sorry, Herb," and kissed him on the forehead in restitution.

After the beer was served the waitress took our food orders. "Would you like liver dumpling soup?" she asked everyone.

Nearly everyone answered, "Yes."

"And what would you like for your meal?" she asked each of us.

Wiener schnitzel, bratwurst, goulash, and German meatloaf were typical answers. After a long enough wait for the preparation of the meals, as we got hungrier and hungrier, the order came out and was served. It was gobbled up between a flood of talking about our youthful days, and current health matters and goings on with our families.

Four of the people in the group that met that day were men, all over 80 years old, but they were as excited as teenagers when we met. Most of them were from my old neighborhood, and went to the same grammar and high schools as I. Bill came with his wife, Genie. Herb came with his wife, Jan, who was from Kansas. They had lived in Michigan, but now have moved back to Kansas this year because of some health problems that Herb has. Dave, a widower whose wife died some years ago, came alone. And of course, I came with my wife, who, as you know, is from Germany.

You will remember from stories I related in the chapter on shenanigans, the activities that Dave, Herb, Norb, Bill and myself participated in when we were teenagers. One of them was about Dave helping me sneak out of the house when I was grounded; another was participating in Halloween pranks together; then there was drinking half-gallon bottles of beer in our cars in the Chicago alleys; and a reckless experiment in drinking booze for the first time on New Year's Eve.

Gang meeting at Brauhaus on Lincoln Avenue for lunch

A trip to Door County, WI with the gang

A bunch of high school friends at Wells Park Gymnasium, 1948

Girl's club at Amundsen High School with
some of the original girls from our group

Also, I joined the Navy for four years in 1951 during the Korean War after Dave and Herb had already joined the Navy earlier in the year. Bill joined the Marines shortly after that, but only for two years.

There were seven women who came to the luncheon. Four of them were widows without spouses, all a regular part of our group. They were married to guys who were part of the original gang of the '30s, '40s, and '50s. Marlene was married to Frank; Rosemary, who now lives in Florida, was married to Bernie; Gene was married to Dick; Mary Lou was married to Glenn. The other three women were with their husbands, Genie and Bill, Jan and Herb, and me and Hanna.

Another female member of the group, Mary, was not present, nor was Larry, a close member of this group, who was a tall, dark, and good-looking guy with an engaging smile, and who moved to California and got married there. Helen hadn't been there for years. She was married to Norb, who died an early death. There were the popular girls in grammar school and high school, the Joans, Audrey, Harriett, Dorothy, Gert, and more, who we often reminisced about, but they were not a part of our group meetings.

It makes you feel good to have and meet these old friends occasionally during the year. The people in our group are friendly, have nice dispositions and seem as though they are from a kinder, gentler, more responsible generation than some people today.

Afterwards we went to a new two-story German/Polish delicatessen a few doors from the Brauhaus, which had a zillion tasty and unusual imported items from Europe. At the end of the luncheon and delicatessen visit, after the escape to our childhoods, we all hugged goodbye and said, "I look forward to seeing you at the next luncheon."

German American Friends

Another major part of our social life and the groups of friends we associate with are the German Americans we know. Hanna and I held our annual Advent dinner at our house every year for over 20 years on the first Sunday in December. Most of the people we invited were Germans, along with several American couples. The party normally started about three o' clock in the afternoon. As the guests arrived, they would have a cocktail, a beer, or a glass of wine and some appetizers. The Manhattan cocktail, made with Southern Comfort, was a popular drink. Later, for dinner we served a typical German meal consisting of potato salad, sauerkraut, German wieners, and Leber Kese. The Leber Kese is a German meat recipe that looks pinkish like baloney, but has a better, more wonderfully distinct flavor.

Hanna and I would worry a bit about how many people would come or not. We didn't know exactly how well attended it would be until later in the afternoon. Even though the bulk of the people arrived on time, some came a little late, and one or two parties, because of other commitments, came a couple of hours late.

Mostly German friends, some American, at the yearly
Advent dinner at our house.

The first guests to arrive at our party and ring our doorbell, of our close German American friends in the Chicago area, were often Toni and Anita. They usually would be followed by Horst and Annie. The next German couple ringing our doorbell often was Hans and Traudl, who were both from the same town as my wife, Bremerhaven, in northern Germany. Traudl and my wife only lived a kilometer away from each other and went to the same grammar school, but didn't know each other until they met here.

The next guest was Kathi, a widow from the original German area of the current Czech Republic. She had one child, a boy, and lost her husband during WWII. She came to the U.S., worked and managed to raise her son on her own, and never got married again. She is an energetic, interesting personality with many friends—and is 87years old! Sometimes she helps me with my gardening.

Another German couple to arrive was Wolfgang and Karen. He also came from my wife's hometown of Bremerhaven. Karen came to the U.S. when she was nine or 10 years old, from a town nearby.

Hanna's sister, Annegret, was a regular at our Advent dinner. She always came early on Sunday to help us get things ready and then stayed to help clean up. Annegret moved to the United States when she was 17 years old, which was a few years before Hanna came. She met and married Fred after she moved here. Fred's parents were bakers. Annegret and Fred had three boys—Tom, Mark, and Tim.

Stephan and Marianne attended many of our Advent dinners. Rudy and Helen came also in the early years, but as they grew older and less able to travel, they dwindled off. Erica and Walter came to the Advent party for many years when they lived in Illinois, but have since moved to Prescott, AZ. Edith, who is actually Austrian and not German, came to the party for many years, but since her husband Walfred died and since she is quite a distance away, she dwindled off in recent years. She, however, was not born in Germany, she is from Vienna, Austria where she met her husband when he was in the service.

There also have been some close American friends who have come regularly to our Advent dinners, one being an old-time friend Frank and his fiancée Sharon. Both Frank and Sharon are widowers who lost their spouses vacationing on a cruise ship. They plan to marry soon and my wife and I will be witnesses at their wedding. Another American couple who attended the Advent parties is Mary Margaret and Tom. They are friends of more recent years and both went to the same high school in Itasca, IL.

Those were the days in December when we enjoyed having friends over during the holidays, who have given us many pleasant memories. Last year was the first Advent dinner we missed in over 20 years, because I broke my hip.

German Friends in Arizona

The cold Chicago winds, the snow and ice, along with the cloudy and dreary days of early January would drive us away to another climate in the winter. So, each year after enjoying our Advent dinner and the Christmas season, Hanna and I would scramble to get ready to go to our winter home in Arizona. Our bags were packed around the third or fourth day of January, and a limousine picked us up to take us to O'Hare Airport. About three hours and 40 minutes after leaving Chicago we'd land in our destination. Usually the sun was shining and the temperature was around 60 to 70 degrees. The warm sun comforted our freezing skin and we would thaw out. We would take a prescheduled van from the airport to our winter home in the town of Surprise, which is a northwest suburb of Phoenix.

Once we arrived we began unpacking and getting the house in order again for our four-month stay, setting up the hot water heater, cable TV, phone, and more. But then, there were always some problems, if not with getting the TV going or getting the ice maker in the refrigerator working. I checked out the car, which was stored in the garage for eight months, to see if it would start. If not, I had to charge the battery up. We usually stuffed some bread, butter, and cold cuts in our suitcases when we left Chicago, either for a sandwich that evening or for breakfast the next morning, and then the next day we did our first big shopping for food.

We also worried a little that we wouldn't be invited as much to dinners and get-togethers as in previous years. The next morning the first call and invitation came in from Renate, a close old friend from the Chicago area. "Welcome back! How was the flight? Everything okay? Do you want to go to breakfast Friday morning?"

"Yah, sure," Hanna answered.

German friends in the Phoenix, AZ area, where we owned a
winter home for 11 years.

Renate was born in Sudetenland, which was part of Germany at one time and then it was given to the Czech Republic after the war. She met her husband Bob, who was in the U.S. Army stationed in Germany, in Garmish Partenkirchen. Bob was born in Boston and they have two children.

Hilde and her partner Herb called us. "Can you come over for a drink Saturday night? We are going to have you over for dinner, but we can't right now. Maybe next week." She was also a close old friend of ours from the Chicago area, who moved to AZ maybe 15 years ago after her husband passed away. She was born in Germany near Frankfort, came to the U.S. in the 1960s, and married Wolfgang, also from Germany. Hilda and Wolfgang had three children. After Wolfgang died she moved to AZ where she met Herb. They became a couple. Herb is an American born of German parents, moved from Long Island, NY, where he worked for the Steinmetz Piano Company as an industrial engineer, to AZ. Herb has become a good friend of ours.

The next call came from another German couple we are close with, Renate and Diethelm. "Can you come over for coffee and cake on Sunday afternoon?" she asked.

"Why, we sure can."

Both of them are from around Dresden in what was once East Germany; they immigrated in the '60s, and settled in Schaumburg, a suburb of Chicago, where they had three sons. In later years they moved to the land of the sun. Diethelm was a master craftsman and has a deeper, crisp German voice with an appealing accent. Both Renate and Diethelm have a certain social charisma.

For many years we also got calls from Inge and Karl and met with them every so often. Karl emigrated from Kiel in northern Germany in the 1960s, lived and worked in the Chicago area for a number of years, and then was transferred to Phoenix, AZ. A few years ago they bought a second house in Illinois to be near their daughter and grandson in the summer and fall. When Inge's husband died she sold her house in AZ and moved permanently back to Illinois to live in the house they had bought there.

My wife got a call from Mimi. "I would like to invite you to dinner on Easter Sunday."

We marked the date on our calendar. It was some time ahead yet. Mimi emigrated from Munich, Germany to Chicago in the 1960s, where she met her husband Jerry, a pharmacist, and had three children. She got divorced some years later, moved to California, worked as a photo re-toucher, and when she retired, she moved to AZ.

Giesela and Rudi always invited us for some good German dinners, but they gave us a chance to settle down for a couple weeks. Giesela would then call and ask, "Are you guys available for a charcoal broiled German dinner at our house on Friday?"

Hanna checked our calendar and saw we were free that day and said we would be there. They are from Germany, came to the U.S. in the 1960s, also lived and worked in the Chicago area and then moved to AZ when they retired.

Some other people we get together with, but not so often, are Rudi and Julie, two people from Austria. Rudi also is a snowbird, like ourselves, living in the same area where we live in Illinois. Rudi is an excellent golfer and a witty guy. He emigrated from Graz, Austria in the 1960s. In the U.S. he was a partner in a successful cabinet-making and carpenter contracting company. There were more social contacts we had with other Europeans in Arizona, but they were not all our closest friends.

Also, our close American friends, Frank and Sharon in Illinois, bought a condo near us a few years ago in Surprise, and we met with then socially while out there, as well as in Illinois.

So, our friends in AZ have kept us busy while being there in the winters. They made it interesting and fun with their lively conversations, along with the sunny and warm weather. Without this social life with friends, things might have been dull out there.

Chapter 24

RAYS OF SUNSHINE ON THE MATURE TREE

"**D**o you want to sell your company when you retire?" Joe asked me one day about a year before I retired. He was a savvy but friendly guy with a disarming smile.

He was in Chicago for a meeting with us to go over the sales of my software. His offices were in Boston and he handled my software programs, which my engineering company developed and serviced, along with a package of his own HVAC products.

Wow, I thought, *opportunity is popping up for some security during my retirement days*. "Sure, I'm interested." I was careful not to sound too excited.

"Think about how much you might want for it and what would be acceptable payment terms to you...then we can talk about it more."

I evaluated what I thought the company was worth and how much I would like. We did talk about it. To start with, the price I told Joe I would like was way over what he wanted to pay, and what he offered me was under my rock bottom price. We evaluated and negotiated all year long. Finally, we came up with an agreeable price and terms and he bought the company. We divided the payment up into three equal parts; one part would be paid initially and the other two-thirds would be paid over the second and third years. All worked well and this was one big ray of sunshine in my retirement years.

Another ray of sunshine was that my yearly earnings in my company peaked out during the last few years of working, which added substantially to the fair amount already in the fund.

So altogether, along with the comfortable chunk of money from the sale of the company, I started off my retirement at age 65 virtually without money worries—certainly for at least 10 or more years, or so I projected, without depleting the fund too much. Little did I know that I would still be going along for another 17 years into my lower 80s. But fortunately this didn't become a financial problem because I was able to keep my total principal about even over the years. That may sound really good on the surface, maintaining an "x" amount of principal for about 17 years, but it really isn't as good as it sounds. The culprit is inflation. Due to inflation, which was an average of about two percent per year since 1996, the principal diminished its purchasing power quite a bit—about 40 percent. So for every $100,000 of value that I had when I retired, my purchasing power has reduced to $60,000 today.

A third ray of financial sunshine in my retirement was that I was covered by Social Security and Medicare. This has been a blessing since 1996. However, on the negative side, to cover the number of illnesses, surgeries, and doctor and hospital bills I have gone through, I have had to pay ever higher and higher supplemental insurance premiums to ensure that the expensive medical costs would be fully covered. Medicare coverage has diminished over the past 17 years and private medical insurance has gone up and up.

Escaping the Frigid Chicago Winters

My wife and I wanted to be in a warmer climate during the winter years of our retirement, and wanted to escape the blustering snow and freezing winds of Chicago. Hence, during the first six years of our retirement we vacationed in Florida for about a month in the winter. However, it was always a hassle to find a nice place to rent for a reasonable price.

For a couple of years we spent a few winter months near Phoenix, AZ, to see how we would fare there. It was nice. We enjoyed the beauty of the Southwest landscaping and architecture, the orange and lemon trees, blue skies, the sunshine and wintertime heat. We could watch the sunrises and sunsets, and see the stars at night. Plus, as I related in the last chapter, we enjoyed the social life with many friends from Chicago who had previously relocated to Arizona.

We liked it so much we decided to buy a house in Sun City Grand and became snowbirds. We looked at three or four dozen houses, but weren't satisfied with any. Hence, we became discouraged and gave up the search. Then, one day while scanning through Sun City Grand's monthly magazine, I saw an ad for an attractively decorated house. I told my wife, "Why don't we just take a peek at it for fun?" We were surprised and delighted. The previous owners did a remarkable decorating job, and it was perfect for a wintertime house. We both looked at each other and knew we'd found a house that we both liked very much—and bought it a day or two later.

It was a nice, bright house, over 1,200 square feet, with sunshine in the morning in the kitchen nook, sunshine around the front of the house during the day, and then on our covered patio later in the day. It had two bedrooms, open adjoining living and dining rooms, an adjacent kitchen, a covered patio and an attached two-car garage. It was attractively decorated, Southwestern style, and was already fully furnished. All we had to do was move in. We bought the house, moved in for four months in the winter, and bought a car to keep parked in the garage when we were in Chicago.

But, as I think Shakespeare once said, "Alas, all sweet dreams must come to an end." Most recently, after breaking my hip at the end of last year and some health issues the past few years, and after 11 years of owning and maintaining two houses, going back and forth, some headaches, and always some hassle involved, we sold the house. Selling the house was sort of a bittersweet experience.

We went back to Illinois, where my family lives—our four children, 12 grandchildren, two great-grandchildren, my two brothers, my wife's sister—all in the Chicago area, but were sad to leave the warm weather and our friends.

A Major Ray of Sunshine

Another major ray of sunshine in both Hanna's and my life, something of great satisfaction and of overwhelming value in anyone's life and family, is having your children turning out all right, having a loving relationship with them, and seeing them raise their own families and children successfully.

Who Won the Battle: The Genes or the Environment?

The German seed of 1931 is running out of its cycle of growth, is aging, and becoming an old tree. So the time has come in these memoirs to look at what perpetuated my growth; the stumbling around at first, and then the successes.

The genetic makeup of the seed and the cultural influences of the German Americans in my life had their affects on me. But so did the American environment and culture that tugged on me as to my choices in lifestyle as I went along.

You might ask, to what extent did the genes in the seed have on me? How did they direct growth and what I became? Basically, the genes in the seed did their job as to the color of my hair, eyes, and skin. They determined my shoe size, how tall I grew, the shape of my nose, and so on. This was based on which genes were the dominant ones between my parents. My basic mental, mechanical, and creative abilities were preconceived in the genes.

But my social behavior, personality, and lifestyle got stretched out this way and that way because of the genes and the culture, which were in conflict. Some of the German genes bounced head-on against the American lifestyle. The more rigid German genetics often crashed into the more easygoing American way of life.

The nature of many Germans involves following the rules, proper social behavior, some rigidity of thinking, and so on. The nature of a typical American seems more relaxed, looser, and more casual. I have found that when a German woman marries an American man, combining their different natures results in their lifestyles being modified somewhat. The woman becomes a little less rigid and more easygoing, and the man a little more disciplined than he might have been. Also, the resulting children of the German American marriages takes on some of the strengths of both sides and fewer negatives.

A principle of evolution of human genes is that they will automatically adapt themselves to the environment over long periods of time. One example is that skin genes have adapted themselves to colder climates and to hotter, sunny climates. The results are pale, light skins and darker skins for protection against the sun. Likewise, an evolution of brain genes was probably brought about by the disciplined learning and thinking in Germany over the centuries. Some German genes may harbor information and the beliefs of ancestors. Personalities could reflect one's ancestors through the evolution of brain genes over time. So, a descendent of German parents may unwittingly reflect some mentality, personality, and characteristics of his or her ancestry.

I think I am a little more rigid and disciplined than I might have been with American parents. The genetic makeup of the seed, nevertheless, was a factor in my life. The German genes may have nurtured differently if I had been born and raised in Germany with the same parents. If the seeds had grown there in a different environment and culture, if this genetic body grew up in the German political circumstances in the 1930s and '40s, the outcome would have been different. However, with the genetic makeup of the seed with the same parents, my physical characteristics would have been basically the same. And my parents' political beliefs and culture were such that we probably wouldn't have been involved in German politics of that era.

But would I have had a mischievous, flighty, slightly sullen childhood in Germany with the social order and discipline there? Probably not!

Life is a Quilt

There are other broader factors that come into play in one's life, such as the patches in your quilt blanket. Many of the patches in my life quilt were rays of sunshine in my life.

Life is a blanket of patches sewn together that reflect the many people who influence a person's life. It is a never-ending blanket that grows bigger and bigger with every year. It is a patchwork of family, relatives, friends, classmates, teachers, coworkers, and bosses. Politicians, businesspeople, and religious leaders make up a part of your patches. Artists, entertainers, actors, and writers also slant our thoughts and beliefs and are patches in one's quilt.

All these groups we are exposed to leave their marks on our lives in varying degrees. They contribute to molding our lives, for better or for worse. Each patch, or each group of patches, has their own unique influence on our lifestyles, choices, reactions, beliefs, behavior, and what we become.

My rigid German mother, who made me keep working while in grammar and high school at 18 different jobs, is a big patch in my quilt. This old guy looks at his quilted blanket and is thankful and happy that most patches were a meaningful part of his life.

What Did We Live Through Since the 1930s or '40s?

Other rays of sunshine in my life were the fantastic changes in science, medicine, technology, lifestyle, and more since the 1930s and '40s. These rays perpetuated my growth and longevity.

- *In Health Care:* Antibiotics…penicillin…sterilized medical procedures. How many times have antibiotics rid me of dangerous infections that might have ended my life early? If you got tuberculosis, pneumonia, or typhoid fever, you had a good chance of dying.
- *Unbelievable Surgical Miracles:* A heart attack and subsequent quadruple bypass almost 25 years ago has kept me alive since then…(plus my wife's good care of me). And technology and

226

medical advances are continuing at a rapid rate even as you are reading this page.

- *Life Spans:* Average life spans have increased from about 50 to 80 years old.

- *Food Preparation:* A person can cook prepackaged meals and heat leftovers in just minutes in the microwave.

- *Shopping:* From small, specialized Ma and Pa stores to supermarkets and malls. Bread used to get stale in a few days without preservatives.

- *Transportation:* Evolution of cars, airplanes, jets, ships, and trains. With cars, my 1938 Ford with mechanical brakes, and the need for constant tune-ups and new spark plugs, to the modern automatic autos today with no tune-ups or new spark plugs needed for over a 100,000 miles. There were no Japanese cars or expressways. Airplanes went from small propeller planes to gigantic 787s. I was able to do my thing by flying all over the United States and Europe in a matter of hours.

- *Space Technology:* Rockets to outer space, the moon, Mars, satellites circling the globe, and space stations.

- *Computer Revolution:* Computers have absolutely revolutioniz-ed the world; instantaneous calculations, unlimited storage of data, unbelievable sources of information on the Internet.

- *Communications:* Cell phones, instantaneous email, faxes, reduction of post office mail.

- *Photography:* I traded my box camera in for a roll film folding camera, then another trade to a 35mm model, and so on until I reached the no film, no processing, and instantaneous digital cameras.

- *Entertainment:* The evolution of movies, television, games, from comic books and Western series movies to roaring, ear-shattering special effects movies; from 15-inch black-and-white tube TVs to 50-inch, crystal sharp flat screen beauties;

music from melody, harmony, and pleasantness to ear-piercing, brain-rattling, screaming, pounding beat pop music, rock, soul, hip hop; amplifiers and electronic instruments.

- *Architecture:* Sky scrapers, hospitals, earthquake-proof structures.
- *Psychology and Psychiatry:* More effective treatments, drugs and therapies for mental, emotional, and relationship problems.
- *Population Growth:* The population of the U.S. almost tripled, growing from 125 to 310 million. The world grew from around one to maybe four trillion. Wow! When will it end?

But on the negative and the dark cloud side of events:
- *Bunch of wars:* WWII, Korea, Vietnam, Afghanistan, Iraq, cold wars, terrorism, suicide bombers, mass murderers. Germany and Japan were two conquered countries, now they are leaders in the industrial world.
- *Devastating Military Equipment:* Atom bombs, drones, supersonic planes, automatic firing rifles, intercontinental ballistic missiles, stealth bombers, radar, and sonar.
- *Natural disasters:* Devastating floods, tornados, earthquakes, horrendous storms, tsunamis, wildfires, and avalanches.
- *Economic cycles:* Depressions, recessions, stock market crashes, heart palpitating up-and-down economic cycles.
- *Government Programs:* We went from no government pension programs (Social Security) and no federal income tax and other taxation for the typical person, to about 40 percent of our earnings...and the country being trillions of dollars in debt and maybe ending up in financial ruin if more effective action is not taken.
- *Human Behavior and Society:* Degradation of family life, marriages, religion, morality, and the sexual revolution. Most people generally believed in God, The Golden Rule, common

rules of behavior, human respect. Christmas was seen as a religious holiday. Drugs and alcohol, from Prohibition to crack. People drank but didn't take drugs much.

Visions of a Dream World

What about a dream world where Mother Nature and human behavior are better controlled? Dare we dream about idealistic things? Take a deep breath before you start reading this. Think of a world where food is plentiful for everyone and starvation is mostly eliminated; where all vegetation grows without insects, diseases, droughts, floods or extremes of heat or cold that ruin the crops; where all human or animal diseases, sicknesses, and genetic disorders are substantially controlled and humans live healthy, satisfying lives to over 100 years. All leaders are fair, kind, passionate, negotiate fairly and intelligently, and are honest; where there are no dictators or oppressive leaders or governments; where wars are avoided; where crime, stealing, and killing is mostly abolished or substantially controlled; where all religions are accepted and respected by each other; where what constitutes moral behavior and what the objectives of life are, is coordinated and mostly agreed upon between the religions; where marriages are more compatible and intelligent, and where families live more in harmony; where the harmful emotions and inaccurate thinking that produce prejudice, stereotyping, intolerance, cynicism, and negativism are mostly controlled.

Okay, now you can breathe again.

Now, you may wonder, how can we achieve these idealistic conditions in the world? Please read on.

If a Truth Serum Were Given to Everyone

The truth is hard to come by, but if everyone could only tell the truth and not lie or fib, most of our problems in the world would be solved. If everyone was vaccinated with a compulsory truth serum and they had to tell the whole truth and nothing but the truth, bedlam would occur at first, Herb Daniels predicted in his *Modern Almanac* column. But I believe that thereafter a newer, better, more trustworthy world would emerge.

- The prices of stocks would plummet at first, and then adjust to their true value.
- Newspapers would fold and newscasters would go off the air, but start over being completely honest.
- Advertising agencies would take nosedives and then resume with only the facts.
- Businesses would be flooded with returns and would change to providing exactly what they claim.
- Union officials would be charged with grand theft, but then manage finances more transparently.
- Perjurers would overload the court dockets for years, but then move along smoothly and quickly.
- Autobiographies and history books would be recalled.
- Used car sales would be revolutionized.
- *Politicians would be speechless or get kicked out of office.
- *Dictators, and power-happy, dishonest leaders would be executed.
- *Many existing marriages would end up in divorce, but new ones would start on a sound foundation.
- *Bureaucrats and lobbyists would lose their influence, and resume with honesty only.

    *These items are not in Herb Daniels's original article. They were added by the author.

And so, this final chapter of these memoirs ends with this positive, hopeful dream. We should make every effort to develop this truth serum as much as we can.

Goodbye for now, aufwiedersen, and good luck to all readers!

Acknowledgements

Many thanks to my youngest daughter, Jamie DeLaCruz, who did the perceptive and valuable initial draft editing and content evaluations.

Many thanks also to my wife, Hanna Wendes, for checking out the accuracy of names, dates and places of people and events, and for giving me her reactions to the many stories in the book helping me to select the most interesting ones.